Each One, Teach One

Preserving and protecting the Second Amendment
in the 21st century and beyond

Fiction by Greg Camp:

The Willing Spirit

A Draft of Moonlight

No Easy Road

If You Want Peace

Each One, Teach One

Preserving and protecting the Second Amendment
in the 21st century and beyond

Ranjit Singh and Greg Camp

Pax Propter Opem Press
Sheridan, WY
2016

© 2016 Ranjit Singh and Greg Camp
All Rights Reserved

All rights reserved. No part of this publication may be reproduced, stored in a retrieval system, or transmitted in any form by any process—electronic, mechanical, photocopying, recording, or otherwise—without the written permission of the publisher and authors.

ISBN 978-1537445410

Printed in the United States

A message from a lawful immigrant and a college professor to all law-abiding American gun owners and to anyone sympathetic to our cause

Dedicated to the intransigent masses in flyover country:

May your spirit of independence forever be a thorn on the side of those elitist busybodies who would plan, control, and micromanage your lives if they could

And to Sharie, who stands with me

Table of Contents

Preface   i

Part I: Getting Started

My Story   3
A Left-wing Academic Becomes a Gun Nut   11
On the Origin of Rights   19

Part II: Ignorance Leads to a Fear of the Unknown

Bra Straps, Barrel Shrouds, and Bliss   29
Propaganda Is Mightier than an AR-15   38
Gun-abstinence Zones   51
Fairy-tale Feminists   58
Of Arms and Men   63

Part III: Fear of the Unknown Leads to Emotional Calls for Action

From Egalitarianism to a New Caste System   73
Asymmetry of Information, Asymmetry of Force   78
Assault and Definition   92
"Do SOMETHING, Please!"   101

Part IV: Knowledge Destroys Ignorance, Familiarity Destroys Fear

Use It or Lose It	121
The Demographic-Knowledge Threat to the Second Amendment	125
A New Evangelism	129
Lawful Immigrant and New Citizen Outreach	134
What About the Rest of the Developed World?	138
Towards a Left-Right Convergence on the Second Amendment	144
Reaching Across the Divide	154
Four Rules of Gun Safety	160
A Non-Aggression Pledge for Trainees	161
A Basic Armory	162
Epilogue	169
Appendix: Political spectra	171
Suggested Reading	176
Index	177

Preface

The book that you're about to read was written by two authors. You picked that up from the title page, but let's be clear about what that means. We—Ranjit Singh and Greg Camp—come from two different backgrounds, have lived different lives, and hold different political views. Ranjit is more in line with Libertarians, while Greg sides mostly with Greens. The chapters were written individually, and they'll have a by-line for the particular author. Note that our views weren't characterized by Republican or Democrat. We both have objections about the corruption and special interest favoritism to be found in the two major parties of this country. One goal of this book is to encourage you, our reader, to think for yourself, to base your positions on principles, not on fancy marketing or polls. Our core principle is that each human being is born with basic rights that were not granted by society and cannot be taken away.

We have a number of disagreements on matters of politics, and that's a good thing to show. Support for gun rights doesn't need to be limited only to one side of the traditional left-right spectrum. And that's our second goal, to build a broad coalition of support across the country so that the idea of a conservative and a liberal working together to defend gun rights no longer sounds like an impossibility.

A third goal is to remind us all that while rights are inherent, they can be violated. As with gun rights, so with all others. Speech, religion, privacy, due process—those and many others are threatened today by the false promise of security, the false fear of the Other, and the false division of American against American. We must come together as citizens of one great land to say that no matter what candidates we support or where we fall on a graph of political views, we all support rights. As Benjamin Franklin once told his fellow revolutionaries, if we don't hang together, we'll all hang separately.

The most effective prefaces are often the shortest. In brief, this book is for gun owners who have friends or family who aren't supporters of gun rights. It's for readers who are considering buying your first gun or who have just made that purchase and wonder about the arguments for and against guns. And it's for open-minded readers who may have no interest in ever owning firearms, but who respect the concept that other people have the right to make their own choices. This book is to get every one of you to teach someone else about the importance of all rights, including gun rights.

Each one, teach one, and thank you for joining with us.

Ranjit Singh and Greg Camp

Part I: Getting Started

My Story

Ranjit Singh

On the 26th of November 2008, I sat at my computer, feverishly refreshing a news web page, trying to get more information on what was happening in Mumbai. All I knew was that there was a big terror attack and that scores were dead. No one said how many terrorists were involved, who they were, or how many sites were being attacked simultaneously. There were explosions in addition to the shootings, and false rumors of attacks on other sites spread like wildfires.

The intelligence and security apparatus of India spanning all levels of government was caught completely off-guard[1]. Officials were in a mad, post-hoc scramble to figure out what was going on. The media frenzy reported one version of "facts," only to be corrected by themselves with another new version, over and over again.

The attacks were an act of war, and everyone was caught in its fog.

I was not directly affected, sitting in the comfort of my home in America. But I have family in Mumbai and was deeply concerned about them. It took numerous attempts to reach them and make sure that they were safe.

It took nearly four days for the attacks to be stopped completely. Those four days were pure hell for the millions of people of Mumbai. The world, or at least most of it, was looking at the city with empathy. Some of my friends feared and wondered aloud about what would happen if such simultaneous attacks were to be committed in their own hometowns.

After the attacks were stopped, the Pakistan-based Islamic terrorist organization Lashkar-e-Toiba—Army of the Pure, in English—taunted the Indian government, saying that they were just a "trailer," and that the impure, dirty, infidel people of India had not yet seen the actual "movie." The implication, of course, was that the Mumbai attacks, which nearly overwhelmed India's intelligence and security apparatus, would be repeated in a much larger assault involving several cities at the same time. The violence would be an order of magnitude greater, leading to ever more confusion and chaos and decreasing the ability of the government to respond.

It should surprise nobody that such evil exists in the world. What should appall everyone, however, is that such evil can and does go unchecked and unpunished. As of this writing, Zaki ur Rehman Lakhvi, the mastermind behind the 2008 Mumbai attacks, is out on bail from a Pakistani prison.

The innocent victims could have been anyone I knew. They could have been my business acquaintances. They could have been my childhood friends or classmates. They could have been my neighbors. They could have even been my own family members. Watching the slaughter made my blood boil. Ideology aside, the terrorists were cowardly bullies who were taking the lives of defenseless people. The impunity with which they were walking around calmly picking out targets was shocking.

About a year after the attacks, I saw Dan Reed's documentary, "Terror in Mumbai,"[2] which shone a bright light on the frail humanity of law enforcement. There were a number of policemen, some armed with bolt-action rifles and handguns, present at the Chhatrapati Shivaji Terminus when the terrorists started shooting people. Most of the policemen froze or retreated into hiding. When the time came to do their duty, many of them failed. This was a betrayal that cost people their lives. To their credit, some of them rallied, fought back against the better-equipped terrorists with the weapons they had, and lost their lives. But most of the killing had already been done by the time the police reacted.

This weakness was not limited to the railway and local police. It was also evident in the delayed deployment of the paramilitary commandos who waited for hours in New Delhi for a plane to fly them to Mumbai and the inordinate amount of time—four days—it took to sweep every site clean. First and foremost, the behavior of law enforcement officers showed a lack of preparedness and a lack of foreknowledge regarding such a ferocious attack.

Lest anyone think that I am being unfairly critical of the intelligence and security apparatus of India, I would like to point out that such incompetence and ineffectiveness exists around the world. American intelligence missed 9/11. Russian intelligence missed the Beslan school crisis, and their armed forces mishandled the subsequent massacre. British intelligence missed the July 7, 2005 bombings. Spanish intelligence missed the Madrid train bombings. Kenyan intelligence missed the Westgate Shopping Mall and Garissa College attacks. French intelligence missed the November 2015 Paris attack. The list goes on. People around the world trust their governments for their security, and their governments fail miserably more often than people realize.

And while governments fail in one of their fundamental functions, they also end up killing a number of innocents without suffering any meaningful consequences. The Indian Army has committed multiple human rights violations, including extrajudicial killings, disappearances, and torture in Kashmir. America's drone strikes have killed over 160 Pakistani children[3], and no one has been held accountable in any way. British agents, in pursuit of suspects of the July 7, 2005 bombings, shot an innocent Brazilian—Jean Charles de Menezes—many times in the head with hollow-point bullets—called "cop-killer" bullets by the sycophantic media—that his face was completely unrecognizable[4]. If non-state actors were to behave in such a way and kill innocents, they would be punished harshly. But governments get away with actions which would bluntly be called crimes if private citizens were to commit them. Governments and their media shills are artful at explaining away the dehumanizing and murder of innocents through euphemisms like "collateral damage."

When the Mumbai attacks were underway, I saw pictures of commandos dressed in black surrounding the Taj Hotel with scary-looking black guns. I knew nothing about guns. I had never handled a gun in real life, and the only guns I saw were cops' pistols that were safely holstered. I never cared to learn about them. I *completely* rejected the notion that civilians have a right to arms, and believed that arms should exclusively be in the hands of the military and police. I was one of the "law-and-order, good-government" types.

However, when the attacks were in progress, a part of me wished that I was one of the commandos in Mumbai, hunting down the barbarians who were committing such a horrendous crime. I wished I had the power to stop the atrocity. It was a natural human reaction that I am sure was being felt by people from different countries, races, and religions around the world. The desire to stop violence against innocents, even if by using reciprocal violence, is something that *any* normal person would have, however nonviolent and peaceable our natural tendencies may be.

The Mumbai attacks changed my outlook in a fundamental way. They changed the way I see government, its purpose, and its relation to citizens. They changed the way I see my adopted country, the United States of America, its Constitution, and its Bill of Rights. They changed the way I see the rural gun-toting "bitter clingers" who are regularly dissed by the American media. They changed the way I react to the snickering and smug condescension towards gun owners I hear in some of my social circles.

Reading several stories of governments failing in their primary function—security—led me to recognize the right to self-defense of every human being in every corner of the world.

The right to self-defense is a corollary to the right to life. It has been largely delegated by most peoples of the world to their respective governments, with the exception of Americans. To paraphrase Founding Father James Madison, Americans have the advantage of being armed, which they possess over the people of almost every other nation on Earth. Governments around the world are afraid to trust their people with arms. But in America, the right to self-defense and its best tool—arms—are protected from the prying hands of government by a fragile parchment barrier.

As I started learning how to handle firearms, I became more comfortable with them. As I researched the history behind the Second Amendment, I became convinced by the idea that ordinary citizens have a natural right to arms. And the more I informed myself on contemporary gun control debates, the more I became convinced that this freedom is especially fragile, and that it is constantly under the threat of being eroded into oblivion.

My personal experience changed from having no knowledge about guns to recognizing the fundamental human right to life, its preservation, and the tools of that preservation. I decided to write this book. Its goal, as the title suggests, is to defend the Second Amendment for generations to come.

As the reader has probably guessed by now, I am an immigrant from India and a naturalized citizen of the United States of America. I am a gun owner.

I live in a very leftist neighborhood in a very leftist city. I work with and move around in social circles comprised of those who call themselves "liberals." There was a time when the term, liberal, implied that someone stood for Liberty. It has not so often been the case for at least a century.

This book espouses positions which a *lot* of my nearest and dearest strongly and vehemently disagree with. They are not evil people. They are good people—the kind of people who would help you in a heartbeat if you ever needed it.

However, in our modern, overly politicized world, politics is a religion, especially for the irreligious. Political discussions ruin what would otherwise be amicable and fruitful human relationships and sometimes end in outright bitterness and hatred.

As a matter of principle, I have ceased discussing politics with my family, friends, and colleagues. My relationships are the foundation of my life, and there is no point in ruining them debating the merits of one candidate or social program over another. In *my* ideal world, society would not be so politicized and few things would be a zero-sum game. Unfortunately, in the *real* world, the government has stuck its grubby paws in just about everything, creating an inevitable bitterness. Fighting over a limited pie is the norm as groups of people try to steer the heavy hand of government to their own advantage—and to the disadvantage of others.

In our modern environment dominated by microaggressions, hurt feelings, and accusations of bigotry at the slightest disagreement, there cannot be a national conversation on anything. A verbal discussion, by its nature, is less accommodating to patient thought. In the hope that the written word will provide more pause to the reader and allow for reason to prevail, I chose to write this book. Lastly, in the hope of not fraying the relationships which form the very basis of my life, I chose a *nom de guerre* that comes from my country of origin.

Notes

1. Trofimov, Yaroslav, Geeta Anand, Peter Wonacott, and Matthew Rosenberg. "India Security Faulted as Survivors Tell of Terror." *The Wall Street Journal*. 1 Dec. 2008. Web. <http://www.wsj.com/articles/SB122809281744967855>.

2. Terror in Mumbai. Dir. Dan Reed. Quicksilver Media, 2009. Film.

3. Woods, Chris. "Drone Strikes in Pakistan: Over 160 children reported among drone deaths." *The Bureau of Investigative Journalism*. 11 Aug. 2011. Web. <https://www.thebureauinvestigates.com/2011/08/11/more-than-160-children-killed-in-us-strikes/>.

4. Dodd, Vikram. "Police used dum-dum bullets on Brazilian shot at tube station." *The Guardian*. 16 Nov. 2005. Web. <https://www.theguardian.com/uk/2005/nov/16/july7.menezes>.

A Left-wing Academic Becomes a Gun Nut

Greg Camp

Picture an academic. For many, such a person will look like Albert Einstein or Carl Sagan, someone with a rumpled mass of hair or elbow patches, someone whose job involves chalkboards and libraries rather than machine tools and dirt under the fingernails. And as Nobel laureate and physicist, Steven Weinberg, has illustrated, the view among academics is often that guns are something best left to the rustic past[1].

As I participate in debates over gun rights, my opponents often doubt that I have spent almost two decades teaching English composition and literature. And things are even less believable in the sense that in many ways, I come from the left end of the political spectrum in America. I explain, too frequently to deaf ears, that I am pro-choice on abortion, in favor of marriage equality, and supportive of renewable energy. I deplore the attempts among fundamentalists to blend religion and state and look forward to a healthcare system that is much more like Canada's. So what on Earth or in the heavens would make me a gun enthusiast?

I am not to the manner born. My parents refused anything to do with guns—cap guns, water pistols, anything that would encourage violent thoughts in a boy. Television programs had to be pure at heart, and we dined on a great volume of plants, since their church, Seventh-day Adventism, required a vegetarian diet. My parents were what Marine Lt. Colonel and firearms instructor Jeff Cooper called hoplophobes, people afraid of the power and responsibility that comes with owning and using guns.

But keeping a child from being exposed to firearms in America is hopeless. My great uncle, Jesse, was taking care of me one day after school when he showed me what I now realize was a .22 caliber revolver that he kept in his home. My second encounter with guns was on the Appalachian Trail. A much larger revolver dangled from the backpack of a man hiking with his son as the two of them passed my family and me. The thought of someone openly carrying a gun fascinated me, but since my parents were against it, that got buried for later days.

As someone who comes at things from the left wing, I adopted the stereotypical position against guns for a long time. In political terms, my ideology is for the common person. This is a perspective that I shall return to in this chapter, but for the moment, it is enough to say that I tacitly assumed that gun control would keep people safe.

But then a student of mine turned in an argument essay on

the Second Amendment. His analysis focused on the writings of liberal constitutional scholars who make the claim that if we treat gun rights as collective, all other rights can be similarly ignored or waved away.

Since I first became politically aware, I have valued the rights protected by the First Amendment. The fundamental right to express myself is key to me as a writer. The humanist and skeptic who has much to say about religion, including some praises for it, is glad that religion and government are separated by law. The argument that protections for speaking, writing, and believing or not believing could be taken away by the many groups who wish to curtail these rights if we take a casual attitude about gun rights woke me up.

This gave me the theoretical basis for supporting gun rights. Two more things pulled me into the exercise thereof. The first was participating in a writers' group with a colleague who wrote stories about Reconstruction Era Tennessee. He and I connected over a mutual enjoyment of traditional woodworking tools—and over the fact that we both belonged in a different century. His writing told the tale of people who lived on the land, provided for themselves, and used machines that were still within the comprehension of the ordinary person. Thanks to his influence, I started writing westerns, and guns are an essential piece of that genre.

The other instigation was an episode of the History Channel's series, *Tales of the Gun*, on the Luger P08. At the time, I was innocent of knowledge about most guns, but the Pistole Parabellum 1908 is one model that is recognizable in an instant, even by someone who knows little else. It is an elegant machine, made in a time when fine tools were hand-fitted works of art.

So I decided to become a gun owner. As an academic and a novelist, I read. I read voraciously, far and wide in what gun blogger Kim du Toit labeled the gun nut forest. Du Toit's website—now gone dark, I am sorry to say—had page after page of images and commentary about guns. I read the work of Jeff Cooper. I read whatever I could find on safe gun handling and skillful use. And then I bought a gun.

My first firearm was a Remington New Model Army, a reproduction of the 1858 cap-and-ball revolver. It came in the mail, since it is an antique design. I loaded it with the recommended twelve grains of FFFg powder, took a two-handed grip, cocked the hammer, and squeezed the trigger.

I had fired guns before—a friend's .22, a relative's Beretta .40 pistol—but I had never been shown how to aim or how to run a firearm. After my reading, I knew Cooper's Four Rules, and I knew what the front and rear sights were for.

The hammer dropped, and the revolver let out a satisfying boom and a cloud of sulphurous smoke. The recoil that I had expected to be heavy was so slight that I fired the next five rounds one-handed. And I was at that moment thoroughly a gun nut.

How does this fit into a liberal philosophy? I have to begin with what being a liberal means to me. A liberal fundamentally believes in liberty. This is not simply a conceit, nor is it merely a historical artifact. Yes, liberals in the Age of Enlightenment are the kind that today's conservatives respect, but modern liberals are no less devoted to liberty than their intellectual ancestors. Liberalism asserts the idea of liberty so much that adherents insist that it be the right of every person.

This means that you have the right to ingest what you wish, to associate with whom you wish, and to do to and with yourself as you please. You have the right to speak your mind, having filled it with whatever beliefs appeal to you. In consideration of that, I will object whenever the government or corporations penetrate too deeply into the private lives of any of us.

I have to make a distinction here between liberalism and the Democratic Party. Political parties, especially in America, are big-tent coalitions that are often as much about tossing goodies to various supporters as they are about acting on principles. In my formulation of the concept, liberalism seeks to protect the greatest liberty for all. That includes making sure everyone has access to education, healthcare, a clean environment, and safe streets. Too often, though, liberals can lose sight of the purpose—namely the empowerment of each person. This is a case of the heart being in the right place, while the head gets lost in minutiae. But liberty is hard to enjoy for someone who is poor, ignorant, or sick, and a concern of liberalism is to overcome those debilities.

So why do I, a liberal, love guns? For one thing, as I suggested above, I appreciate the applied science of firearms. Their design and function can be learned in an afternoon of reading about and examining the instruments by almost anyone, but they can reward a lifetime of study as well. They are not mysterious black boxes to which one submits questions and receives answers by magical and apocryphal processes. They are machines that are simple enough to be accessible, but complex enough to remain challenging. In this respect, my enthusiasm is more in the nature of the tinkerer and hobbyist than in political ideology, but I love the freedom to participate in the hobbies of my choice.

I also love guns for their demonstrative power, as I discovered in shooting the first gun I bought. At fireworks displays, I am thrilled by the concussive points of white light more even than the splashes of color. I enjoy bagpipes for their unapologetic volume. In the same manner, firearms create a satisfying and demanding moment of *Sturm und Drang*. My black powder revolver booms out with a mighty voice and cloudy breath. My 1911 is no more of a conversationalist than a guard dog, but it cannot be misunderstood, and my Mosin Nagant rifle is a loud display of the idea that we all have to get our start somewhere. Silence has its valued place, but thunder borrowed from the gods that can be held in the hand can banish a world of cares. And thunder in this case is a form of speech. It is the shout of the citizen, a declaration that the serf cannot make.

And guns are excellent instruments for securing the democracy of power. Firearms—along with their cousins, the longbow and the pike—forced the demise of aristocracy. Whoever first said, "God created man, but Sam Colt made him equal," understood my point. I love guns for the distribution of power that they make possible. Any time the mighty are compelled to take a moment of pause is a reason for celebration, and guns are one means of achieving this. The birth and growth of the Internet and the promise of 3-D printers points to a future in which personal liberty can be more and more widely distributed till one day, every person is free. That may sound utopian, and it is. But the higher we set our goals, the higher we can climb.

I am a liberal, and I want you, my reader, to own a gun. I want you to own it thoroughly, which includes devoting yourself to its study and practice. Whatever position you take on the political spectrum, I want you to have the means to defend yourself against anyone who would try to stand above you—whether ordinary criminal or would-be tyrant. The question of gun ownership does not properly divide political parties; it separates the diffident and the lazy from the strong and the individual.

How each of us arrives on the side of gun rights is not important for those rights themselves, and it is up to each one of us, whether liberal or conservative, moderate or radical to work together on this area of agreement and to bring in more people of all backgrounds and philosophies. That is the only way that we can secure this right that we value.

Notes

1. Zadrozny, Brandy. "Nobel Prize-Winning Texas Professor: Guns Not Welcome In My Class: A legendary physicist has vowed to defy, if necessary, Texas's campus carry bill that would allow concealed weapons in the classroom." *The Daily Beast*. 28 Jan. 2016. Web. <http://www.thedailybeast.com/articles/2016/01/28/nobel-prize-winning-texas-professor-guns-not-welcome-in-my-class.html>.

On the Origin of Rights

Greg Camp

In debates over who should be allowed to own and carry firearms and what firearms if any they ought to be able to obtain, one key point of contention is the subject of rights. Is it a basic human right to be in possession of a gun at home or in public, or is that a privilege that only certain people ought to be granted?

Consider the language used to describe rights. Often, people use words like grant or create, as in saying, for example, that the Obergefell ruling in 2015 granted the right to marry to same-sex couples. The assertion made here is that the Supreme Court's majority, following developments in state law and public opinion, decided that gays and lesbians deserve to be given the same benefits in taxes, insurance, property, and so forth that straight couples gain when they are legally married, rather than recognized a right that such couples already possessed.

This is the consensus view of rights, the belief that rights are something we agree to, whether consciously and purposefully in laws or simply assumed to be the case in the culture. An example of this is found in the Seventh Amendment to the Constitution. A right to a jury trial is guaranteed for all suits over matters exceeding twenty dollars. This is clearly something that is created by agreement. After all, units of money called dollars—in fact, money itself—are the product of a society, not something fundamental in nature. A similar case is found in contracts. Such a document lists out obligations of the parties involved, but also the rights formed by the agreement.

In cultural assumptions, consider behaviors that seem natural to us on the basis of the particular society we live in. In the United States, it is socially normal to find shirtless men at beaches, while women typically have their breasts covered. Exceptions to this are becoming more common, but they still are shocking to many Americans. By contrast, in many places in Europe, women at the seashore go uncovered. Geeky boys used to look forward to the latest issue of the *National Geographic* in hopes of seeing photographs of islanders in the South Pacific in the days before the Internet, having little hope of seeing the genuine article any time soon.

This sounds like a discussion of social mores, but consider the attitude of a man who goes shirtless at the beach. It is likely that this is something he has not given much thought to, but if asked, he might claim that doing what he does is his right.

The problem with the consensus view is that what society giveth, society may take away, blessed be the name of society. Consensus is something that can come and go. In America since 9/11, the right to believe and practice a religion has been challenged—if your religion is Islam. Attempts to ban the construction of mosques in Murfreesboro, TN[1] and in New York City[2] illustrate this. Would the right to belong to a religion that many hate at present survive a vote? If basic rights are subject to agreement, they will last no longer than public opinion supports them. I have watched the shift in attitudes toward gay marriage over the last two decades with joy, but the idea that the private lives of my fellow human beings is subject to popularity is something that should disturb anyone who values freedom.

Another notion of the origin of rights is that they are given to us by God. On the face of it, this seems to have been the view held by Thomas Jefferson, expressed in the Declaration of Independence in the statement that our rights are endowed by our Creator. But this ignores the nature of political language, the need to phrase things in a way that appeals to the public. Jefferson was at most a deist and probably an atheist, as can be seen in his private letters and actions. Using religious concepts garners more support among voters, but he took pride in not having a theology department at the University of Virginia, told the Baptists of Danbury, Connecticut that there is a wall of separation between church and state, and refused the ministrations of a clergyman at the end of his life.[3]

Are rights, though, the gift of a deity? This may be a view that religious people wish to hold, but it creates trouble if we are not ourselves believers or when we talk to those who do not belong to the same theological club. It also leaves rights up to interpretations of religious texts. More significantly, it does not actually answer the question. Why would a deity give us a particular list of rights? If that gift was an act of arbitrary whim, we are back to something no better than the consensus view, other than adding in a loudest voice in the process of reaching agreement. If rights are made for us on the basis of some rational process, we can refer ourselves to the reasoning without worrying over who may or may not have done it.

So what are we left with? Human beings are born able to make choices. Too often, the question asked is why ought we to be allowed to act, whereas the appropriate question is to inquire as to what business anyone has in telling us not to. I may regard my neighbors as silly for being vegans or for putting shiny hubcaps on their cars, but it really is none of my concern. Going back to Jefferson, in his book, *Notes on the State of Virginia*[4], in Query XVII, he states, "The legitimate powers of government extend to such acts only as are injurious to others. But it does me no injury for my neighbor to say there are twenty gods, or no god. It neither picks my pocket nor breaks my leg."

As long as my actions do not force others to take part, what reason can anyone offer for making my decisions for me? This is John Stuart Mill's harm principle, an idea similar to the one Jefferson expressed. If what I choose to do is not hurting an innocent person, I must be free to do as I please. It is possible to quibble endlessly over what we mean by harm. An unprovoked killing of a human being is seen by just about everyone as wrong, but what about slurs against minorities? What about playing a car radio at high volume in the night? What about smoking marijuana in the privacy of one's own home? The line that distinguishes harmless from harmful will be debated over and over, but to reasonable people, the general concept should be clear.

The law in a free society is an expression of the will of citizens, but it neither creates nor takes away the autonomy of each person. When the law is just, it protects that autonomy. In other words, it protects rights. An unjust law has no claim to the title of law at all. It is merely force.

What, then, can we say about guns? Guns are objects and have no rights themselves, but as objects, they can be property. And the ownership of property, acquired fairly in a way that does not harm innocents, is a natural right. So is self-defense, and guns are the current best means for protecting innocent lives.

Advocates of gun control often pose the question that if we have a right to guns, do we want the government to give them out to everyone. This is a confusion about the nature of rights, again. To say that we have the right to possess guns does not mean that they must be given to us. It means that we can buy or make them out of our own resources. In the same way, we can regard universal healthcare as a good social policy—from the liberal point of view, at least—but not as a right, since it is provided by taxation and must therefore come about through the agreement of voters. To sum this up, I have the right to give something to myself or do something for myself, but if I want you to give to me or do for me, I have to ask. I have no justification for demanding.

The belief that rights are inherent in human nature was held by the founders of the United States. Look at the Bill of Rights. The assumption in the language is that the fundamental rights enumerated already exist. The First Amendment forbids Congress from making laws restricting the exercise of religion or speech. The Second Amendment identifies the people as having the right to keep and bear arms, but that right is taken as already existing, one that cannot be infringed. The Ninth Amendment reminds the government that enumerating some rights does not mean that the people have given up any rights not specifically named.

Even if the concept of natural rights, rights that are inherent to every human being from birth, is unsatisfactory on philosophical grounds, in pragmatic terms, it is the view that best defends both individual liberty and a free society. In numerous debates, journalist and public intellectual, Christopher Hitchens issued a challenge to his opponents to name any society grounded in humanist principles, the principles described here, that has become a tyranny. By contrast, he pointed out the many societies in which rights are doled out by a ruler, whether secular or religious, that became totalitarian. And one key principle of humanism is inherent rights.

The American experiment in liberty is dependent on our commitment to individual rights, rights that we each are born with. If politicians cannot trust us with guns, we have to wonder what other choices they will want to deny us. If we remain vigilant, we will never have to find out.

Notes

1. Brown, Robbie and Christine Hauser. "After a Struggle, Mosque Opens in Tennessee." *The New York Times*. 10 Aug. 2012. Web. <http://www.nytimes.com/2012/08/11/us/islamic-center-of-murfreesboro-opens-in-tennessee.html?_r=0>.

2. "Obama defends right to build mosque near 9/11 site." BBC. 14 Aug. 2010. Web. <http://www.bbc.com/news/world-us-canada-10973459>.

3. Note that at present, atheists are less trusted than rapists, according to one poll:

   Bailey, Ronald. "Are Atheists Worse Than Rapists? Polls find that godless Americans are (still) wildly unpopular." *Reason.com*. July 2012. Web. <http://reason.com/archives/2012/06/27/are-atheists-worse-than-rapists>.

4. Jefferson, Thomas. *Notes on the State of Virginia*. Ed. William Peden. New York: Norton, 1954. Print.

Part II: Ignorance Leads to a Fear of the Unknown

Bra Straps, Barrel Shrouds, and Bliss

Ranjit Singh

What is the shoulder thing that goes up?

If you were to ask ordinary people on the street, there is a good chance that their answer will be a bra strap. But that is not the answer you would get from enthusiastic gun control proponent and US Congresswoman, Carolyn McCarthy. When pressed by a TV interviewer to explain what a barrel shroud was in the context of a rifle ban bill she co-sponsored, Rep. McCarthy explained that it was "the shoulder thing that goes up."[1]

Wouldn't you expect someone who was working on taking away other people's freedom to know what he or she was actually banning? Imagine the outrage if our congresscritters tried to ban Dihydrogen Monoxide without knowing that they were banning water[2].

When gun controller and US Congresswoman Diana DeGette was asked on live TV about her bill banning magazines that could hold more than fifteen rounds, she explained that such a ban would result in high-capacity magazines quickly going out of circulation because they were not reusable[3]. This is what she said:

> These are ammunition, they're bullets, so the people who have those now, they're going to shoot them, so if you ban them in the future, the number of these high-capacity magazines is going to decrease dramatically over time because the bullets will have been shot and there won't be any more available.

Think about that. Someone who had no idea that a magazine is reusable was trying to ban them, believing that they were for one-time use only. DeGette's staff tried to spin her stupid comments by saying that the Senator meant to say "clips" instead of "magazines," adding to the mockery she was being subjected to.

US Congresswoman DeGette is from Colorado, the state which passed a series of feel-good gun control measures in early 2013 in the wake of the Aurora, CO and Newtown, CT shootings. These gun control measures[4] were sponsored and passed exclusively by Colorado Democrats[5,6] in a highly divisive vote with a narrow total of 18-17 in the Senate and 34-30 in the House. As reported in *The New York Times*, several politicians who voted for these measures were ignorant of how firearms work, and were given on-the-job training by none other than Colorado State Senate President John Morse himself[7].

> Mr. Morse's hand was on the tiller during much of that debate. A former police chief, he said he found himself in a position of not just rounding up votes, but actually explaining the mechanics of guns to fellow Democrats. He brought a magazine to show his colleagues how it worked.

The new restrictions provoked a political reaction which led to the recall of Morse and of fellow senator, Angela Giron. Another senator—Evie Hudak—resigned when faced with a likely recall.

The ultimate award for ignorance rightfully belongs to California State Senator Kevin de Leon, who has authored or sponsored legislation requiring ammunition permits and even fingerprinting and recording the driver's license information of people who buy ammunition. At a press conference decrying 3D-printing technology, Senator de Leon spouted the following incoherent, garbled nonsense[8]:

> This is a "ghost gun." This right here has ability with a thirty-caliber clip to disperse with thirty bullets within half a second. Thirty-magazine clip in half a second. You have this weapon, which is an automatic sniper weapon that is used by our troops in the military in Afghanistan.

The judicial branch has had its own gaffes on the subject of guns. Supreme Court Justice John Paul Stevens, one of the four dissenting justices in the closely-decided *District of Columbia vs.*

Heller and *McDonald vs. City of Chicago* cases, wrote an opinion piece in the Washington Post on April 11, 2014 titled "The five extra words that can fix the Second Amendment", in which he called for adding the words "while serving in the militia" to the Second Amendment[9]. The goal of such a change is to let the government take away everyone's guns and hide them somewhere until they are needed for militia service. In this article, Justice Stevens described the weapon used in the tragic massacre at Sandy Hook Elementary School as an "automatic." This error was also made in Justice Stevens's book, titled, *Six Amendments: How and Why We Should Change the Constitution*[10]. Justice Stevens served as an intelligence officer in the U.S. Navy during World War II and presumably must have experience with firearms. Given that, was this error merely a "typo," or did one of the nine important people in black robes entrusted with interpreting the Second Amendment not know the distinction between automatic and semiautomatic firearms? Is someone who is recommending the restriction of the right to arms "while serving in the militia" actually unfamiliar with the very arms he wants the US government to take away from its citizens, or did he merely mix up words despite his legal background which demands the precise use of words? In fairness, the term, automatic, used to refer to any firearm that loaded a new round into the chamber through the recoiling of the action, but Stevens should be aware that the meaning of the term has changed since the first half of the twentieth century. It must also be noted here that in the aforementioned article, Justice Stevens also used the weasel phrase "assault weapon," whose meaning has been distorted over time and misused with the express purpose of confusing the public[11].

It is not just legislators or judges who seem to be ignorant of firearms. This ignorance extends to the executive branch as well. President Obama, who bragged about skeet shooting "all the time" and had a fantastical photo-op with a shotgun in 2012, described the weapon used in the tragic massacre of school children in Sandy Hook Elementary School as "fully automatic" at a fundraiser[12]. Was this a mere error, or did a Harvard Law graduate, former president of the Harvard Law Review, and a professor of constitutional law not know the distinction between a fully automatic and semiautomatic weapon?

Ignorance may be bliss to some, but in reality, ignorance leads to an irrational fear of the unknown. How many people in power really know firearms? How many of them have actually owned them, handled and operated them? Do they come from backgrounds like mine where guns are simply not part of the culture and quite possibly frowned upon? Is it that these people in key positions of power are merely ignorant and therefore biased against an important freedom because of their unfamiliarity with it?

Should every candidate for public office be asked about their *experience with and ownership of firearms*, as opposed to their *position on gun rights or gun control*? Someone with a reasonable amount of experience with guns will be less likely to recoil (pun intended) at any mention of gun rights than someone who has no experience and is therefore ignorant. This is especially important given the repeated congressional infringements upon the right to armed self-defense.

The judiciary is supposed to strike down anything unconstitutional, but similar to the legislative branch, there is a significant risk of bias arising from ignorance. Does the Supreme Court's "liberal" contingent comprising of Justices Breyer, Ginsburg, Sotomayor, and Kagan have any personal experience with guns? Justices Ginsburg, Sotomayor, and Kagan are New Yorkers, and New York City is quite possibly the worst place in America for those who believe in gun rights[13]. (You can't even own a taser in the great state of New York.[14]) How much of an influence does such a cultural background have on their interpretation of the Second Amendment? Is a New Yorker who has never touched a firearm in his life and believes that the right to arms should be restricted to militia service going to empathize in any way with the security and self-defense concerns of a gun-owning rural Iowan who gets pathetic cell phone reception and whose closest neighbor is a mile away?

What about the lower rungs of the federal judiciary? What about state legislatures and state judiciaries? How much of an influence is the cultural background of elected representatives going to have in the future as they move from the state to the federal scene while advancing in their so-called "careers"? If an elected official can deftly explain the difference between a frappuccino, macchiato, latte, and a mocha, but can't tell the difference between a round, bullet, caliber, and a magazine, what implications will it have for gun rights?

Notes

1. Leghorn, Nick. "BREAKING: Carolyn McCarthy (D-NY), of 'Shoulder Thing that Goes Up' Fame, To Retire." *The Truth About Guns*. 8 Jan. 2014. Web. <http://www.thetruthaboutguns.com/2014/01/foghorn/breaking-carolyn-mccarthy-d-ny-shoulder-thing-goes-fame-retire/>.

2. "Dihydrogen Monoxide--DHMO Homepage." *DHMO.org*. 12 Aug. 2016. Web. <http://dhmo.org/>.

3. Sullum, Jacob. "Congresswoman Does Not Realize the 'Assault Magazines' She Wants to Ban Are Reusable." *Reason.com*. 3 Apr. 2013. Web. <http://reason.com/blog/2013/04/03/congresswoman-does-not-realize-the-assau>.

4. Colorado (State). Legislature. House. CONCERNING PROHIBITING LARGE CAPACITY AMMUNITION MAGAZINES, 2013. *Colorado State Legislature*. Web. <http://www.leg.state.co.us/clics/clics2013a/csl.nsf/fsbillcont3/7E6713B015E62E6F87257B0100813CB5?open&file=1224_enr.pdf>.

5. "HB 1224 - Limits Firearm Magazine Capacity - Voting Record Colorado Senate." *Vote Smart.org*. 11 Mar. 2013. Web. <https://votesmart.org/bill/votes/

43113#.V65MtaIy2GZ>.

6. "HB 1224 - Limits Firearm Magazine Capacity - Voting Record Colorado House." *Vote Smart.org*. 13 Mar. 2013. Web. <https://votesmart.org/bill/votes/43115#.V65NrqIy2GZ>.

7. Healy, Jack. "Colorado Lawmakers Ousted in Recall Vote Over Gun Law." *The New York Times*. 11 Sept. 2013. Web. <http://www.nytimes.com/2013/09/11/us/colorado-lawmaker-concedes-defeat-in-recall-over-gun-law.html?_r=0>.

8. McCluskey, Brent. "California senator explains the dangers of a 'ghost gun' (VIDEO)." *Guns.com*. 20 Jan. 2014. Web. <http://www.guns.com/2014/01/20/senator-de-leon-tries-explain-dangers-ghost-gun-video/>.

9. Stevens, John Paul. "The five extra words that can fix the Second Amendment." *The New York Times*. 11 Apr. 2014. Web. <https://www.washingtonpost.com/opinions/the-five-extra-words-that-can-fix-the-second-amendment/2014/04/11/f8a19578-b8fa-11e3-96ae-f2c36d2b1245_story.html?utm_term=.98982ac1e082>.

10. Stevens, John Paul. *Six Amendments: How and Why We Should Change the Constitution*. New York: Little, Brown and Company, 2014. Print.

11. See:

    "Conclusion." *Assault Weapons and Accessories in America. Violence Policy Center.* 1988. Web. <http://www.vpc.org/publications/assault-weapons-and-accessories-in-america/assault-weapons-and-accessories-in-america-conclusion/>.

12. Tapper, Jake. "Obama flubs gun used in Sandy Hook." *CNN.* 4 Apr. 2013. Web. <http://thelead.blogs.cnn.com/2013/04/04/obama-flubs-gun-used-in-sandy-hook/>.

13. "New York Gun Laws." *NRA-ILA.* 11 Jan. 2016. Web. <https://www.nraila.org/gun-laws/state-gun-laws/new-york/>.

14. Taylor, Daniel. "Is It Legal to Use a Taser for Personal Protection?" *FindLaw.com.* 30 Sept. 2014. Web. <http://blogs.findlaw.com/blotter/2014/09/is-it-legal-to-use-a-taser-for-personal-protection.html>.

Propaganda is Mightier than an AR-15

Ranjit Singh

Everything about the ignorance of public officials—whether they are legislators, judges, or executives—applies to the media and its opinion makers as well. Opinion makers can be more dangerous than rulers, because the former wield the mighty pen, whereas the latter merely wield a sword.

Any news item or opinion piece, when strained through a filter of ignorance and unfamiliarity, will result in the propagation of dangerous ideas which take a life of their own. Lies and half-truths when repeated a thousand times and amplified by short attention spans and 140-character limits in the ignorant echo chamber of modern social media will become incendiary "truths" that proliferate through the world while the actual truth is still getting its boots on.

Most journalists claim to be politically independent and nonpartisan. Even if you disregard the dishonest or agenda-driven among them, it is still a fact that every journalist (and every human being for that matter) has some form of implicit bias which seeps into his or her work and life. Their claims of independence must be weighed against their ownership of or experience with firearms. How many of them are truly familiar with guns as opposed to merely (or barely) familiar with the jargon involved? If you wouldn't trust a celebrity gossip reporter with no scientific background in the reporting of complex scientific news, why would you trust a reporter with no knowledge of firearms with reporting news relating to weapons?

Consider the case of Huffington Post reporter Ryan J. Reilly. While covering the Ferguson riots in 2014, he tweeted a picture of bright-orange ear plugs and asked his Twitter audience if they were rubber bullets[1]. Or the case of CNN Tonight's Don Lemon, who incorrectly claimed that he could buy an "automatic" rifle in under twenty minutes and doubled down on his erroneous position even after his guest Ben Ferguson called him out on it[2].

Another example of media bias comes from Wes Siler of *Gizmodo.com* who thought he had a "gotcha" moment when he found a video of Texas Senator Ted Cruz carrying an unloaded break-action shotgun with the action open and barrel pointed back[3]. Siler, aware of his own lack of firearms knowledge, interviewed a "local hunter and NRA member" and used this sole person's comments as a basis for an embarrassing article which was quickly panned on-line[4].

Each One, Teach One

CNN

The Gold Medal for Ignorance goes to America's alleged "Newspaper of Record," *The New York Times*. In a story discussing President Obama's skeet shooting hobby, reporters Peter Baker and Mark Landler misidentified the gun used as a rifle, not a shotgun[5].

Pete Souza/The White House

After publication, the following embarrassing correction was appended to the article:

> Correction: February 2, 2013:
>
> An earlier version of this article misstated the type of weapon that President Obama fired in a photo released Saturday by the White House. It was a shotgun, not a rifle.

Note the use of the word, misstated, instead of misidentified in the correction; the former is associated with an error in speech, the latter is associated with the absence or incompleteness of knowledge. *The New York Times* cannot confront its own ignorance when it comes to firearms. After all, *NYT* reporters are well-educated, sophisticated, cosmopolitan know-it-alls.

In light of the above glaring example of ignorance, it should be noted here that on December 4, 2015, the day after the San Bernardino terror attack, the editors of the *Times* published a front-page anti-Second Amendment diatribe titled "End the Gun Epidemic in America"[6]. This was their first front-page editorial since 1920[7]. Short on specifics and long on emotionality, this article called for a goodie-bag of foolish, utopian, impracticable policies, including gun and ammunition bans and confiscation:

> It is past time to stop talking about halting the spread of firearms, and instead to reduce their number drastically—eliminating some large categories of weapons and ammunition.

The gifted wordsmiths at the *Times* used great phrasing to mask their desire for straight-up confiscation by deftly avoiding the word "taking," and instead mixing and spacing the words "require to" and "give up" in one sentence, as seen in this excerpt:

> It is possible to define those guns in a clear and effective way and, yes, it would **require Americans** who own those kinds of weapons **to give them up** for the good of their fellow citizens.

This ignorance, coupled with its malevolent anti-Second Amendment obsession, is also evidenced by its jumping the proverbial gun in incorrectly reporting that the NRA prohibited functioning guns at its 2015 National Convention in Nashville, Tennessee[8]. The NRA didn't have such a prohibition, but a specific arena hosting musical concerts did. When taken to task by other media outlets[9], the *Times* issued an erroneous correction, instead of fully retracting the article and admitting its mistake[10]. In less flattering words, the *Times* abused, and continues to abuse, its power as a major media outlet with over 2.1 million subscribers[11] and 23 million monthly US website visitors by lying and failing to properly correct its lie when caught.

The media's hoplophobic bias is also revealed in "The Great Passive Voice Cop-Out" when it comes to guns[12]. A gun does not auto-magically "go off" unless basic firearm safety rules are callously flouted or the gun has a major mechanical defect. Yet I have come across numerous news articles where passive voice phrases like "gun went off" and "weapon was discharged" are used in an affront to basic common sense. A Google News search for the phrase "gun went off" returned about 7.1 *million* search results as of this writing.

When not driven by ignorance, journalists often parrot talking points put out by anti-Second Amendment organizations without critical examination or context. How many times has *The New York Times* written articles parroting numbers from the Violence Policy Center, a "gun safety research organization," as compared to quoting numbers directly from the National Rifle Association?[13]

I have seen far too many articles about how America leads the developed world in firearm-related *deaths*, without breaking the numbers down into *suicides* and *homicides*. When some articles do break down the numbers into suicides and homicides, they fail to acknowledge the 800-pound gorilla behind firearm homicides: drug prohibition and its glaring consequence of gang turf wars over drug distribution territory. This is a repeat of the early 20th century's foolish, failed experiment with alcohol prohibition and the ensuing gang violence of that era.

I have also seen far too many articles that state that America leads the developed world in *firearm-related* homicides, without providing the important context of *non-firearm-related* homicides. This is a very critical context that is often intentionally left out. Most, if not all, technology is dual purpose. You can use the world's oldest technology - fire - to cook a delicious meal for someone or to burn a nightclub full of young people to death[14,15,16]. You can use a knife in food preparation or to stab people, even entire families to death[17,18,19,20]. You can use a baseball bat for recreation or for bludgeoning someone to death[21]. You can use machetes in agriculture or to hack someone to death. Let's not forget the machete-driven Rwandan genocide with 1 million casualties[22]. You can use pesticides to boost your agricultural yield or to kill yourself the way farmers in India sometimes do when their crops fail[23].

When I see articles that express concern about *firearm-related* suicides in America, I cannot help but wonder why that concern is not applied to *non-firearm-related* suicides. Guns don't cause suicides. Japan, which has a gun ownership rate of 0.6 guns/100 people, has a suicide rate that is 92% more than America's[24] with its gun ownership rate of 112.6 guns/100 people[25]. The Indian state of Sikkim has a suicide rate that is 188% more than America's[26]. India has a gun ownership rate of 4.2 guns/100 people.

Another important subset consists of *medically-assisted* suicides, which are generally supported by the Left. As medically-assisted suicides slowly become legal in more countries, we are encountering unforeseen consequences such as the assisted suicide of a physically healthy twenty-four-year-old woman in Belgium[27]. I recognize that suicide is a problem given its finality. Having seen suicides in my own extended family, I believe that people who are at risk deserve our compassion and help. I even support medically-assisted suicide for the terminally ill. However, I find the disproportionate emphasis on gun suicides to be a hypocritical feint by agenda-driven groups with the sole intention of pushing restrictions on firearms ownership. Is it merely that some people find guns icky, but are comfortable with syringes, ropes, poisons, knives, tall buildings, bridges, and other sundry means of suicide?

Unfortunately, the media's reporting of news related to firearms and gun rights leaves a lot to be desired. The opinion makers in the media are often ignorant, biased, or a combination thereof. Their reporting misshapes the views of people against the fundamental human right to self-defense. Given the millions of people they reach and given how loud their voices are in comparison to an average dissenting citizen, uninformed and misinformed opinion makers can be very dangerous to Liberty. If unchallenged with the truth in the uniquely American environment of free speech, their ideas can do more harm to freedom than any armed force ever can.

Notes

1. McCluskey, Brent. "Reporter mistakes earplugs for rubber bullets, tweets pic." *Guns.com*. 18 Aug. 2014. Web. <http://www.guns.com/2014/08/18/reporter-mistakes-earplugs-for-rubber-bullets-tweets-pic/>.

2. Cooke, Charles C. W. "Don Lemon, Automatic Weapons, and the Integrity of Language." *National Review*. 21 Aug. 2014. Web. <http://www.nationalreview.com/corner/385956/don-lemon-automatic-weapons-and-integrity-language-charles-c-w-cooke>.

3. Siler, Wes. "Hey Ted Cruz, You're Holding Your Gun Backwards." *IndefinitelyWild*. 3 Nov. 2015. Web. <http://indefinitelywild.gizmodo.com/hey-ted-cruz-youre-holding-your-gun-backwards-1740325931>.

4. Weingarten, Dean. "Does Ted Cruz Know How to Carry a Shotgun?" *The Truth About Guns*. 4 Nov. 2015. Web. <http://www.thetruthaboutguns.com/2015/11/dean-weingarten/does-ted-cruz-know-how-to-carry-a-shotgun/>.

5. Baker, Peter and Mark Landler. "President Claims Shooting as a Hobby, and the White House Offers Evidence." *The New York Times*. 2 Feb. 2013. Web. <http://www.nytimes.com/2013/02/03/us/politics/obamas-skeet-

6. Editorial Board. "End the Gun Epidemic in America." *The New York Times*. 4 Dec. 2015. Web. <http://www.nytimes.com/2015/12/05/opinion/end-the-gun-epidemic-in-america.html>.

7. Goldfarb, Zachary A. "N.Y. Times calls U.S. gun laws 'national disgrace' in first front-page editorial since 1920." *The Washington Post*. 5 Dec. 2015. Web. <https://www.washingtonpost.com/news/wonk/wp/2015/12/05/the-new-york-times-has-rare-front-page-editorial-calling-u-s-gun-laws-a-national-disgrace/>.

8. Editorial Board. "No Firing Pins, Please, as the N.R.A. Gathers." *The New York Times*. 10 Apr. 2015. Web. <http://www.nytimes.com/2015/04/10/opinion/no-firing-pins-please-as-the-nra-gathers.html?_r=0>.

9. Mikkelson, David. "National Trifle Association: Rumor: The NRA banned the carrying of guns at their own national convention." *Snopes.com*. 10 Apr. 2015. Web. <http://www.snopes.com/politics/guns/nraban.asp>.

10. Davis, Sean. "The New York Times Is Blatantly Lying About Guns at the NRA Annual Convention." *The Federalist*. 10 Apr. 2015. Web. <http://thefederalist.com/2015/04/10/the-new-york-times-is-blatantly-lying-about-guns-at-the-nra-annual-convention/>.

11. Yu, Roger. "USA TODAY, WSJ, NYT are top three papers in

circulation." *USA Today*. 28 Oct. 2014. Web. <http://www.usatoday.com/story/money/business/2014/10/28/aam-circulation-data-september/18057983/>.

12. Southern Beale. "Journanimalism: The Passive Voice Gun Dodge." *Southern Beale*. 28 Mar. 2013. Web. <https://southernbeale.wordpress.com/2013/03/28/journanimalism-the-passive-voice-gun-dodge/>.

13. Almendarez, Jolene. "I shouldn't have to wait 20 months for a gun." *The Ithaca Voice*. 25 Aug. 2015. Web. <http://ithacavoice.com/2015/08/ithaca-voice-reporter-i-shouldnt-have-to-wait-20-months-for-a-gun/>.

14. Dobnik, Verena. "NY Marks 25th Anniversary of Social Club Fire That Killed 87." *NBC New York*. 25 Mar. 2015. Web. <http://www.nbcnewyork.com/news/local/New-York-Happy-Land-Social-Club-Fire-25th-Anniversary-297489251.html>.

15. Anderson-Minshall, Diane. "Remembering the Worst Mass Killing of LGBT People in U.S. History." *The Advocate*. 24 Jun. 2013. Web. <http://www.advocate.com/crime/2013/11/15/remembering-worst-mass-killing-lgbt-people-us-history>.

16. Castle, Stephen. "Fire in Swedish disco kills 60 Arson fear after 60 die in disco fire." *Independent*. 30 Oct. 1998. Web. <http://www.independent.co.uk/news/fire-in-swedish-disco-kills-60-arson-fear-after-60-die-in-disco-fire-1181746.html>.

17. Associated Press. "Man stabs 14 family members to death before hanging himself." *New York Post*. 28 Feb. 2016. Web. <http://nypost.com/2016/02/28/man-stabs-14-family-members-to-death-before-hanging-himself/>.

18. Nickeas, Peter, et al. "Six found slain in Gage Park home, including child: 'We don't know what happened.'" *Chicago Tribune*. 4 Feb. 2016. Web. <http://www.chicagotribune.com/news/local/breaking/ct-multiple-people-dead-southwest-side-20160204-story.html>.

19. Demick, Barbara. "Chinese attacker kills 7 children, 2 adults with meat cleaver." *Los Angeles Times*. 13 May 2010. Web. <http://articles.latimes.com/2010/may/13/world/la-fg-china-school-attack-20100513>.

20. Reuters. "At least 50 reported to have died in attack on coalmine in Xinjiang in September." *The Guardian*. 1 Oct. 2015. Web. <https://www.theguardian.com/world/2015/oct/01/at-least-50-reported-dead-in-september-attack-as-china-celebrates-xinjiang>.

21. "Cops: Husband bludgeoned wife to death with bat." *HLNTV.com*. 13 Aug. 2015. Web. <http://www.hlntv.com/video/2015/08/13/louisiana-former-deputy-accused-beating-wife-death>.

22. BBC. "Rwanda genocide: 100 days of slaughter." *BBC*. 7 Apr. 2014. Web. <http://www.bbc.com/news/world-africa-26875506>.

23. Gunnell, David and Michael Eddleston. Suicide by intentional ingestion of pesticides: a continuing tragedy in developing countries." *International Journal of Epidemiology*. 32.6 (2003) 902 - 909. Print.

24. "Suicide." *World Life Expectancy.com*. 2014. Web. <http://www.worldlifeexpectancy.com/cause-of-death/suicide/by-country/>.

25. "Annexe 4. The largest civilian firearms arsenals for 178 countries." *Small Arms Survey.org*. 2007. Web. <http://www.smallarmssurvey.org/fileadmin/docs/A-Yearbook/2007/en/Small-Arms-Survey-2007-Chapter-02-annexe-4-EN.pdf>.

26. See:

    Mangar, Nirmal. "Helpline fails to curb suicides in Sikkim." *The Telegraph of Calcutta*. 10 Sept. 2013. Web. <http://www.telegraphindia.com/1130910/jsp/siliguri/story_17331083.jsp#.V66wl6Iy2GY>.

27. O'Gara, Eilish. "Physically Healthy 24-Year-Old Granted Right to Die in Belgium." *Newsweek*. 29 Jun. 2015. Web. <http://europe.newsweek.com/healthy-24-year-old-granted-right-die-belgium-329504?rx=us>.

Gun Abstinence Zones

Ranjit Singh

The most powerful opinion makers are not the ones in the media, but those working in schools. A talking head on TV is powerful, but his power is *nothing* compared to that of an authority figure standing in front of a classroom, who can influence pliable young minds profoundly and change the very course of history.

There is a reason why education, traditionally a function of voluntary society, is now a stranglehold of the government. After all, it is far easier and cheaper to "educate" children in government-run schools than it is to "re-educate" adults in government-run camps.

"Educating" a child to be an obedient, freedom-averse, gun-phobic serf is much easier than forcibly disarming an informed, suspicious, armed adult. The former can be done in the light of day without anyone noticing, and quite possibly with parental gratitude, while the latter can only result in great tumult.

There is obviously no Grand Conspiracy to turn children into obedient serfs. There is, however, a dangerous feedback loop underway in government-run schools that is cutting into America's tradition of Liberty.

This can be seen in the tide of political correctness that undercuts free thought and speech, such as the teaching of "micro-aggressions" to sixth graders[1]. This can be seen in the excessive punishments meted out to children who merely chew pop tarts into guns[2] or point their fingers at their friends and say, "Bang!"[3] This can be seen in the hypersensitive accusations of bigotry to shut down debate at the mention of something as simple as meritocracy[4]. This can be seen in the increasingly common "trigger warnings" and "safe spaces" provided to *adult* college students[5].

Government schools, like most things involving government, have a strong zero-sum aspect to them. Parents with differing opinions on education have no choice but to get involved in pitched battles against one another. I am not talking merely about the fight over teaching creationism in government schools. This happens even over little things like whether elementary school children should get touch-screen devices, and if yes, how much screen time they should get, and so on.

The zero-sum fights over social issues in government schools are often won by the secular left. The losers often are the religious, who are also taxpayers. Government schools, built and operated with funds collected from both secular and religious taxpayers, are invariably secular to the detriment of the religious. As an irreligious person, I am perfectly happy with my children being taught evolution. I know that it is scientifically correct, and I would have a problem if my children were taught biblical stories in a science class. But I bemoan the fact that my religious next-door neighbor is affected negatively by governmental interference into his religion-oriented parenting. I want to live and let live, but the government turns my neighbor and me into gladiators in the "public" school colosseum.

The zero-sum games don't end with the evolution-creationism divide. Homosexuality is still very controversial, despite the full legality of same-sex marriage. Many parents are uncomfortable exposing their children to it. But government schools will teach small children the subject, whether parents like it or not.

The Left has also won the zero-sum sex education fight. Religious parents, who would prefer abstinence-only education, lost. The Left, which is confident in its intellectual superiority to the point of smugness, mocks and routinely derides the "regressive" views of religious parents who have honest, heart-felt, moral objections to pre-marital sex and believe that giving detailed sexual knowledge to an eight year-old is inappropriate and against their wishes.

What is perplexing about the Left is its pushing of abstinence when it comes to guns. The way religious people want their kids to have an abstinence-only sex education, leftists want their kids—and everyone else's kids—to have an abstinence-only gun education. If imparting knowledge of safe sex in government schools is important enough to ride roughshod over the honest concerns of the religious, why is imparting knowledge of the safe handling of firearms anathema? If sex education has no effect on the sexual behavior of school children and does not influence what behavior children perceive is expected of them, why would a rigorous education on firearms affect their general behavior with respect to the use of firearms?

Schools are not merely gun-free zones. They are gun-abstinence zones. An important aspect of the American tradition of Liberty is not taught there. In fact, children are often taught outright that that the very tools which won America's freedom are bad. My children were taught *every single article* of the United Nations Universal Declaration of Human Rights[6] instead of the United States Bill of Rights at their elementary school. The notable difference between the two documents is that the UN's Declaration does not mention any sort of right to keep and bear arms.

It is important to note that schooling is not the same as education and that education is not the same as erudition. Public education does not require government-run schools; in fact, public education through private means is an arguably better option which will satisfy most people and still won't leave poor children behind.

But with the Insatiable Left now shifting the goalposts of government's purpose to "universal Pre-K," also known as government daycare, parents who want to raise their children the way they wish should be especially vigilant and fight this attempt to dismember the family further and make the government the mother and father of all children. If the government cannot be forced out of education, which is the most critical aspect of our children's development, parents should take an active role in the development of their children at home. Any loss of such vigilance will eventually lead to the exercising of tyranny over young minds in the name of societal good.

If there is one institution which is representative of the risk of a future decline of America, it is the government school. The fight to preserve liberty for younger and unborn generations should begin there.

Notes

1. Heise, Steve. "Microaggressions Have No Place in School." *Teaching Tolerance.* 10 May 2013. Web. <http://www.tolerance.org/blog/microaggressions-have-no-place-school>.

2. "'Pop Tart' suspension should be upheld, school official says." *CBS.* 1 Jul. 2014. Web. <http://www.cbsnews.com/news/examiner-recommends-school-board-uphold-pop-tart-suspension/>.

3. Campbell, Andy. "6-Year-Old Suspended for Pointing Fingers in the Shape of a Gun." *The Huffington Post.* 6 Mar. 2015. Web. <http://www.huffingtonpost.com/2015/03/06/6-year-old-fingers-shape-of-gun-suspended_n_6813864.html>.

4. Allahpundit. "Newest campus microaggression: 'I believe the most qualified person should get the job.'" *Hot Air.* 17 Jun. 2015. Web. <http://hotair.com/archives/2015/06/17/newest-campus-microaggression-i-believe-the-most-qualified-person-should-get-the-job/>.

5. Agness, Karin. "Dear Universities: There Should Be No Safe Spaces From Intellectual Thought." *Time.* 11 May 2015. Web. <http://time.com/3848947/dear-universities-there-should-be-no-safe-spaces-from-intellectual-

thought/>.

6. "The Universal Declaration of Human Rights." *United Nations*. Web. <http://www.un.org/en/universal-declaration-human-rights/>.

Fairy-tale Feminists

Ranjit Singh

Left-feminists favor greater government intervention in just about every facet of American life, with the exception of abortion, of course. Left-feminists rarely, if ever, acknowledge accomplished women like Margaret Thatcher, who advocated limited government (also called "Power to the People" in some circles). It should be noted that this behavior is not gender-specific. Leftist men are equally responsible for demanding greater government empowerment over us and glossing over the accomplishments of those who stray from their version of acceptable *goodthink*.

Besides favoring governmental intervention, left-feminists deplore the portrayal of women in weak roles in art, film, and literature. They find any depiction of women as Damsels-in-

Distress, flailing their arms and screaming for a (male) Knight-in-Shining-Armor to rescue them to be grossly wrong and morally repugnant.

As someone who firmly believes in the equality of all human beings on all dimensions—be it race, gender, religion, nationality, or sexual orientation—I am happy that popular culture has adjusted over time to cast women in stronger roles. However, it boggles my mind that left-feminists, while chastising the Damsel-in-Distress trope in the imaginary world of popular culture, have no problem having *all* of us—women and men—becoming Damsels-in-Distress in the *real* world, screaming for our modern-day Knights-in-Kevlar-Armor to come and rescue us from threats. They deplore the feminine plea for help to a patriarch in art, but accept a disarmed victim's 911 call for help to an armed government agent in real life.

If gun violence is so bad as to warrant the political goals of decreasing gun ownership or limiting guns to the military and police, why is gun violence committed on screen acceptable if done in equal or greater parts by a strong female character? Is it not highly acrobatic *doublethink* to deplore gun violence in real life while cheering gun violence committed by strong women on screen?

The right to self-defense with arms is especially important for people facing asymmetric odds against a physically powerful opponent. More often than not, this means a female victim facing a physically stronger male perpetrator. When such is the case, why is it that left-feminists often consciously choose to stay unarmed, and demand that the *choice* to arm oneself be taken away from everyone else?

Why do left-feminists criticize waiting periods for abortions as a sign of "patriarchy," but are comfortable demanding waiting periods for gun purchases? On what ground can one claim that the latter policy prevents impulsive acts of violence, while adamantly denying the same logic with the former?

Consider the case of Carol Bowne, a thirty-nine-year-old hairdresser from New Jersey who was being stalked by a violent ex-boyfriend. As the abusive lout's behavior became increasingly threatening, this law-abiding citizen took all lawful steps necessary for her protection—she took out a restraining order against him, installed a security system and cameras in her home, and also applied for a permit to buy a handgun for self-defense. The State of New Jersey supposedly has a thirty-day processing time for handgun permits, which in reality is a government-induced waiting period and *time tax*. More often than not, in violation of New Jersey's permitting guidelines, permits takes several months to get processed. In the case of Bowne, the permit was not processed even after eight weeks of waiting. This led to tragic consequences. She was *stabbed* to death in her own driveway by her lunatic stalker on June 3, 2015[1]. The culprit was clearly a man, but left-feminist women have an undeniable contribution in the formulation and continued existence of New Jersey's patriarchal firearms laws that infantilize women and men alike.

The pathetic attitude of those who call themselves "feminists" can be seen in former Colorado State Senator Evie Hudak, a native of New York and a "liberal" Democrat. During a March 2013 legislative hearing about a bill banning concealed carry weapons on Colorado college campuses, rape survivor Amanda Collins testified against the bill, describing her painful memories of rape and how she wished she had been armed to defend herself. Ms. Collins was a concealed carry permit holder and was familiar with firearms. Hudak gave a condescending, patronizing response to Collins, saying that "statistics were not on her side" and that "the gun would have been used against her," citing numbers from an unrelated study on domestic violence[2]. If a male legislator had said the same thing, would left-feminists have resorted to their usual verbal jujitsu and accused him of "mansplaining"? Sadly, Hudak's ill-conceived notion that the universal human right to armed self-defense must be subjugated because of "statistics" is not uncommon among left-feminists.

Again, as is the case with hoplophobic legislators, judges, executives, and opinion makers, are left-feminists merely ignorant of firearms? How many left-feminist writers, artists, and bloggers have actual experience with firearms? Does their fear and loathing arise merely from ignorance?

Notes

1. Cooke, Charles C. W. "The Deadly Consequences of Draconian Gun Laws." *National Review*. 5 Jun. 2015. Web. <http://www.nationalreview.com/article/419400/deadly-consequences-draconian-gun-laws-charles-c-w-cooke>.

2. "Colorado Sen. Evie Hudak disrespected rape victim." *The Denver Post*. 6 Mar. 2013. Web. <http://www.denverpost.com/2013/03/06/colorado-sen-evie-hudak-disrespected-rape-victim/>.

Of Arms and Men

Greg Camp

Spend much time in gun control debates, and the subject of male anatomy will arise in arguments made by those who oppose rights. This has even earned the status of a law—Markley's Law, the observation that the longer a conversation about gun rights goes, the probability that someone will make an *ad hominem* attack regarding the gun owner's penis size approaches one.

There is an easy association between guns and penises, and whenever things feel that obvious, it is best to question the assumed connection. Yes, Freud did list firearms as one of many symbols for male anatomy in dreams—though he did not actually say what he is so often quoted as saying about fear of weapons as a sign of retarded emotional and sexual maturity—but then, what did Freud not associate in this way?[1] And while there may be some hard wiring of imagery in our psychological equipment, the usage of symbols is also something we acquire by culture and by appreciation.

Here we must recognize that guns are strongly woven into what it means to be an American. This much may sound obvious enough to be trite, but consider this point in detail. The quintessential genre of this country is the western. It encapsulates everything good about us and so many of our flaws. We are explorers, conquerors, rugged individualists who also are generous with friends, and deeply prejudiced exploiters who can be opened to new ideas.

Do you have a picture here? If your image is not John Wayne, I have to wonder why. He was for a long stretch of the twentieth century the definitive American man, played out as the frontiersman, gunfighter, soldier—the stock characters of masculinity. And of course, again and again, he was armed, usually with a Colt Single Action Army revolver and a Winchester 1892 lever-action rifle, the definitive American guns, so long as we include the M1911. He is everything that T.S. Eliot's character, J. Alfred Prufrock, is not.

Eliot was an American poet who emigrated to Britain and was a part of one stream of Modernism that favored a world-weary elitism, brought to a kind of life by Prufrock—in other words, the opposite of John Wayne. The latter is not so well regarded these days. He is treated as a joke among intellectuals and a fossil to those swimming in what is popular.

Many conservatives decry the shift in our culture that has moved us away from the warrior or cowboy as the typical American. But have things fallen away from some classical masculinity? The claim certainly is made that America has become more feminine, but this is a simplistic take on the shifts in our culture. Instead, we have come to accept a greater variety of interpretation of what being male or being female means. We do not have to be stereotypes anymore.

What does all of this have to do with guns, though? The Roman poet, Virgil, began his epic, *The Aeneid*, with the line, "I sing of arms and the man." His poem is a piece of propaganda on the foundational myth of his empire and one of the cases in which political writing also is great literature. But it is in addition an illustration of how the possession of weapons was assumed to be the act of men. Unless we are talking about Amazons, but they were seen as a strange case, an exception to be marveled at. Some of the goddesses of the period were warlike. Minerva is a goddess of both war and wisdom who emerged fully formed from the forehead of her father, and Diana is the goddess of the hunt, armed with a bow. Both goddesses are virgins, standing outside the traditional roles of women.

In any case, being armed has been something associated with men for a long time, probably going back to our huntergatherer origins. The generality can be stated as men carried the spears and hunted large game, while women carried baskets to gather berries. This is hard to defend in every detail or in every case, but as a general rule, it holds as a concept. Though while we are on the subject of stereotypes and traditional picture of the roles and habits of men and women, it is worth noting that women likely invented beer.[2]

Must we accept things as our ancestors interpreted them? That would be a fallacy, the belief that because something has existed or been done for generation upon generation makes it right. Human beings through much of our existence have seen torture as not only permissible but as entertainment, the subjugation of women and defeated enemies as appropriate to their social structure, and the concentration of divinely given authority in the hands of the few. The beginnings of the modern world are found in our climb out of these horrors, and for too many, that ascent has yet to happen.

In the discussion on the origin of rights, I touched on the subject of agency, but it deserves more development here. Owning a gun is itself a choice, but doing so makes many choices possible. As advocates of gun control point out, this is the power of life and death. But that is the reality for anyone who is capable of making autonomous decisions. When I drive, I have to accept the risk that either through accident or negligence, I might kill someone or someone might kill me. When I cook food, I have to accept that my home—and those of my neighbors—may be burned down. This list can go on and on.

What gun ownership does is confront us with this truth that many would like to ignore. Being a responsible gun owner is the equivalent of taking out the earbuds and putting away the glowing screens while maneuvering in public.

Agency is a key concept in modern political thought. We who support gun rights need to encourage as many as possible—especially including groups not traditionally associated with gun ownership—to join the cause. Exercising gun rights has the symbolic value of an unambiguous statement on rights generally. While we speak, worship, and read often out of habit, and since people around us do these actions themselves in the same manner, we may not have our attention drawn to the wonder of being able to make these choices freely. But owning and carrying firearms these days is treated by many as extraordinary, and as much as I hope this particular right will return to something seen as normal, for now, we have the advantage of being reminded exactly what we are doing.

As someone who values rights, I want good people, regardless of sex, orientation, religion, or ethnic origin to participate, too. This means that I have to commit myself to reject all stereotypes about gun owners. I am obligated to refrain from using racist or sexist jokes or language generally. I have the job to invite new shooters to the community. And I hope you will join me.

Notes

1. Camp, Greg. "A gun is just a gun." *Guns.com*. 20 Jan. 2016. Web. <http://www.guns.com/2016/01/20/a-gun-is-just-a-gun/>.

2. Britten, Nick. "Men owe women for 'creating beer.'" *The Telegraph*. 30 Mar. 2010. Web. <http://www.telegraph.co.uk/news/newstopics/howaboutthat/7538264/Men-owe-women-for-creating-beer.html>.

Part III: Fear of the Unknown Leads to Emotional Calls for Action

From Egalitarianism to a New Caste System

Ranjit Singh

America is egalitarianism in action and has been egalitarian since Thomas Jefferson's lofty declaration that "All men are created equal." Despite the abject evil of slavery, which should never have been part of a country founded on the principles of liberty and justice, America has set the gold standard for the world to emulate since 1776. A surprisingly wide range of world leaders from Vietnam's Ho Chi Minh to India's constitutional architect, Bhimrao Ambedkar, have been inspired by the American Declaration of Independence and the U.S. Constitution. (What their respective countries did with that inspiration is a different story, however.)

Nothing illustrates American egalitarianism like the

constitutional recognition of the universal human right to self-defense. The fact that every law-abiding woman and man, regardless of race or class, can use tools to defend life and liberty is truly marvelous, representative of American exceptionalism.

Most countries around the world restrict the tools of self-defense to a Select Militia in the form of military and police. The Select Militia, in reality, is the *Kshatriya* or warrior caste of the infamous Hindu caste system. It is elitist by its very nature and concedes that some people are simply "more equal" than others. On the other hand, the American concept of a militia, to paraphrase James Madison, is composed of the body of the people[1]. It is egalitarian in essence.

It should be noted here that the Hindu caste system was initially based on the division of labor, and the notion of caste was a fluid one. However, over time, castes became hereditary and ossified, as parents taught children their specialized trades and occupations and society as a whole adopted the asinine idea that one's birth determined the person's occupation, place in society, marriage partners, treatment of others, and treatment received from others.

If ignorance and a fear of firearms gradually grow over the next hundred years and enable a rashly-enacted restriction of arms to a Select Militia, it is not hard to imagine the formation of a hereditary warrior caste in America over the course of time. The morally repugnant caste system of ancient India will make its way into American society and will fundamentally alter the egalitarian character of America.

It is imprudent to be completely dependent on others, especially when its comes to one's security. And it is not just individual defense that is at stake with such dependence, but the common defense as well. History is chock full of examples of what happens when a Select Militia fails, from the Siege of Baghdad in 1258 (estimated 200,000 to 800,000 dead)[2] to the Rape of Nanking in 1937 (300,000 dead)[3]. India's own history may have turned out differently if Hindu society had been egalitarian and not restricted the job of common defense to the men of the warrior castes, and had allowed all men, and in a modern sense, women, to bear arms.

The modern spectre of Islamic terrorism must awaken everyone to the dangers of a complete dependence on a Select Militia. As terrorism becomes more diffuse, pervasive, decentralized, and completely unpredictable, the common defense must decrease its dependence on a Select Militia comprising of the military and police and increase its dependence on the militia of the body of the people to become diffuse, pervasive, decentralized, and equally unpredictable to the violent perpetrators.

Distributed warfare calls for distributed defense. The *individual* natural right to armed self-defense is also the best guarantor of the *common* defense. Americans have the unique advantage of having a right to self-defense that is protected from infringement. This right must be used to its full advantage in the common defense. Only then will America not see a Mumbai, Westgate Shopping Mall, Garissa College, Beslan, Paris, or other large scale terror attack with horrendous civilian casualties.

Islamic terrorists have repeatedly shown their lack of compunction by taking civilian lives in their pursuit of global domination and intolerant subjugation of "infidels." The calculating scoundrels go after low-security soft targets rich with unarmed victims with a single purpose - maximizing the body count. This has happened repeatedly around the world in several countries, especially over the past decade. All Americans must make note of this and demand an immediate end to further infringements on the natural right of self-defense.

It must be noted here that the same goal—maximizing body count—is also pursued by fanatics of other stripes, such as white supremacists, right- and left-wing extremists, and school shooters. The achievement of that perverse goal can only be thwarted by the application of immediate, reciprocal, proportionate use of force, and *ordinary citizens*, trained to arms, are best suited for this purpose.

It doesn't matter if a condescending Ivy League preppy thinks poorly of a saggy pants-wearing ebonics-accented inner-city dweller or a tobacco-chewing tattooed country redneck. That every law-abiding citizen has a natural right to self-defense, irrespective of the elites' disgust and contempt towards them, is a basic, egalitarian, American principle. Restricting this freedom will essentially move America from its roots in egalitarianism to a new casteism, under which, a Select Militia of military and police, combined with a high caste of politicians, politically-connected individuals, and the wealthy will be the only people allowed to possess firearms. The mystique surrounding guns, which is already prevalent in some American subcultures, will spread to the majority of the populace. And when that happens, a proud, free, people will become a cowardly bunch lacking the courage and spirit of their forebears. Freed from the threat of any meaningful resistance, the government can and will push people around in unimaginable ways. Those willing to resist will not have the tools to do so and will have to choose submission over rebellion.

Notes

1. Hamilton, Alexander, John Jay, and James Madison. *The Federalist*. New York: Modern Library, 1937. Print.

2. Alkhateeb, Firas. "The Mongol Invasion and the Destruction of Baghdad." *Lost Islamic History*. 17 Nov. 2012. Web. <http://lostislamichistory.com/mongols/>.

3. BBC. "Scarred by history: The Rape of Nanjing." *BBC*. 11 Apr. 2005. Web. <http://news.bbc.co.uk/2/hi/asia-pacific/223038.stm>.

Asymmetry of Information, Asymmetry of Force

Ranjit Singh

The Founders of the United States created a Bill of Rights to clarify and ensure that certain rights would never be infringed upon by the government. It was meant to underscore the revolutionary idea that the people live in an Ocean of Rights containing mere islands of governmental powers. Unfortunately, the Bill of Rights is now often interpreted as saying that the people live in Islands of Rights surrounded by an ever-rising ocean of governmental powers.

This perversion of American Liberty has slowly crept into our daily vocabulary. How many times have you heard someone say that the "First Amendment gives us the right to free speech," or the "Second Amendment grants us the right to arms," instead of saying that the people have *natural rights* to speech and arms and that the Bill of Rights emphasizes that *the government shall not infringe* on these natural rights? It has been less than 250 years since 1776, and people seem to have already forgotten the purpose of government as described in the Declaration of Independence: That to secure these rights, Governments are instituted among Men.

The growth in the power of the government is startling and must raise the hackles of every citizen. The most dangerous implications of the growth in the government's powers lie in two asymmetries that have developed between the government and the people—the Asymmetry of Information, and the Asymmetry of Force.

In blatant violation of the Fourth Amendment, the government has implemented ubiquitous surveillance programs, whose full scope is not known to ordinary citizens. This has led to the government's ability to spy on any citizen, at any time, and even go back in history to dig up records stored in vast data centers. The government knows a *lot* about us and may well soon know *everything* of importance.

At the same time, the people don't know a lot about the government. The media, who are supposed to be reporting on those in power, have to beg for information and often threaten a lawsuit under the Freedom of Information Act (FOIA). It is important to note that a FOIA request is no guarantor of information. The government can completely reject requests under the pretext of national security[1], or redact any and all useful information to make a response worthless for most purposes.[2] The people know *very little* about the government.

At the government's end of this obnoxious Asymmetry of Information is an eternal quest for even more data. Data is a bureaucrat's crack cocaine. Control freaks can't function normally if they don't fully understand what they are trying to control. The more data that the government collects, the more power its agents have and the more tempted they will be to interfere by force to achieve whatever ends they deem important, whether or not the ends are truly good for the people.

This dark side of data collection leads to abuses by the government and other parties and the negligent loss or purposeful leakage of those data. The government is not made up of ever-angelic, honest, hard-working politicians and bureaucrats. It is made of ordinary people whose minds can and do get addled and corrupted by even the slightest bit of power. There are several cases in recent history of how data has been abused by the government. The NSA's awesome databases and surveillance power have been abused by its employees to spy on their romantic interests[3]. The IRS's power has been abused by both Republicans and Democrats in the past to go after their political opponents[4]. During the 2008 presidential election cycle, a man calling himself Joe the Plumber was subjected to illegal searches in Ohio's law enforcement[5], motor vehicles[6], and family services databases[7] by some petulant pro-Obama government employees and contractors for having the audacity to ask the then senator a question on small business policy. Even former government agents aren't exempt; a Minnesota female ex-cop was subjected to law enforcement database searches for being too physically attractive[8].

These are only the stories we hear. The reason the illegal searches of Joe the Plumber were investigated was because Joe became an overnight celebrity, and someone had the moral rectitude to report the wrongdoing. If you are not a celebrity and happen to be a middle-class schmuck who unknowingly crosses a random government official for some trivial reason, what are the odds that searches of your name will ever be publicized or investigated? You may be subjected to whatever abuse petty bureaucrats can hurl at you, without knowing who is responsible for your harassment and why they are doing so.

One of the big news stories as of this writing is a hack of the Office of Personnel Management, ostensibly by the Chinese government, that has resulted in the loss of important information of around 22 million U.S. citizens who have worked in or applied for jobs with the federal government[9]. This is a really nasty hack because of the broad range of information from performance reviews to information on security clearance that was stolen. Reports indicate that up to 5.6 million fingerprints may have also been taken[10]. The government, in all of its glorious ineptitude, collected this data and acted as a poor steward.

Another big news story from the recent past is a hack of the Internal Revenue Service in which hackers stole over 334,000 taxpayer files[11], over three times the initial estimate of 100,000 files[12].

Given the risks associated with data in general, one can only imagine what risks any registration of guns and gun owners could bring. Once control freaks get a hold of information about us, they will be tempted to use those data to push, coerce, intimidate, and dominate the people involved. The mere availability of data is temptation enough, but when combined with the ever-growing power of the government, abuse will be certain to follow.

It is not just the government that can abuse data. After the Newtown massacre, *The Journal News*, a Gannett-owned newspaper, used *lawful* means to obtain and publish the information on pistol-permit owners in Westchester and

Rockland counties in the State of New York[13], going so far as to create an on-line interactive map listing names and addresses[14]. The paper explained its rationale by saying that its readers were understandably interested in knowing about guns in their neighborhoods.

Imagine the outrage if something similar had been done on any other matter. What if abortions were required to be registered under the law, and some newspaper had requested and published a "slut-shaming" list of women who had had that procedure? After all, a significant percentage of the country thinks that abortion is an act of violence, while supporting the act of owning inanimate objects like guns.

In a world dominated by power-hungry governments, it takes a rare kind of modesty to refuse data collection. Sir John Cowperthwaite, Hong Kong's Financial Secretary between 1961 to 1971, abolished the collection of economic statistics to hobble government busybodies from intervening in the Hong Kong economy. The economic miracle that unfolded in limited-government Hong Kong[15,16] is deeply contrasted by the utter disaster just across the border in Communist China,[17,18] which abated only when Deng Xiaoping's reforms were introduced in the late 1970s.[19,20,21] Communists are the ultimate control freaks who, with all the data and political power in their hands, produced what is quite possibly the greatest humanitarian disaster of the 20th century. It is no coincidence that communists don't like guns in the hands of dirty proles. They *must* have all the data, political power, and guns in their hands so that they can bully their subjects around, treating them like lab rats while performing Josef Mengele-style experiments on entire societies under their control.

In stark contrast to the modesty of Sir John Cowperthwaite

lies the outright arrogance of billionaire busybody Michael Bloomberg. Since the Newtown massacre, Bloomberg has funded groups averse to the natural right to self-defense. His obsession with gun control is exceeded only by his obsession with sugar control. Bloomberg, as Mayor of New York City, called for a ban on the sale of sugary soda bottles that could hold more than sixteen ounces. (High-capacity "assault" sodas, anyone?) Hypocrites like Bloomberg who are supporters of abortion apparently think that "my body, my choice" does not apply to individuals' sugar consumption choices. Surrounded by *gun-toting* bodyguards, the last thing that he would like when he issues his imperial Sugar Edicts is an unwashed white redneck or black inner-city undesirable *toting a gun* and *refusing to obey* his micromanaging, megalomaniacal orders. In fact, Bloomberg was reported by the Aspen Times to have openly called for seizing guns from inner-city minority males in the 15-25 age range, and then moved to block video footage of his comments.[22] There is a link between control-freakishness and gun-control-freakishness, and men like Michael Bloomberg are the best example of it.

Some people think that gun rights activists are a bunch of tinfoil-hat wearing crazies when we claim that gun registration is the first step to gun confiscation, but the concerns are valid. History has shown that data of *any* sort will be abused, encouraging control freaks to push people around. *Gun registration data is no different.* The oft-quoted historical examples of gun registration and confiscation from the Weimar Republic in Germany and Turkish-subjugated Armenia should rout the progressive hoplophobes' rainbows-and-unicorns beliefs that "No one wants to take away your guns." Regardless of what hoplophobes claim or believe, politicians will be tempted to deputize *men with guns* to take away *other people's guns* once ownership data is available.

The Asymmetry of Information between the government and the people is only exacerbated by the Asymmetry of Force. The US government has the strongest military in the world. Law enforcement at various levels internally are also heavily armed and have become slowly militarized as they have adopted the equipment and tactics of the Department of Defense. This sort of power, in bad hands during bad circumstances, can lead to terrible human suffering.

As technology progresses and weapons become mechanized and fully autonomous, the government's hand will only strengthen. This will further worsen the asymmetry of force between the government and the people. And with politicians—who are a lot more likely to be lying sociopaths than an average citizen, having the power to unleash such force on the people with minimal repercussions—it is hard not to conclude that freedom will be in peril. This may not happen immediately, but the risk of it happening over a century or two is not something that can be dismissed out of hand as a mere conspiracy theory.

In the midst of this vast asymmetry of force, the persistent demand by hoplophobes to further disarm the populace by way of "common sense gun safety regulations" is truly scary. Guns are *the* constitutional circuit breaker. The only real check on governmental power is the sheer force that people have, and once the last vestiges of the citizenry's armed might are removed, all bets will be off.

The rainbows-and-unicorns hoplophobes have forgotten that government is neither reason nor eloquence, but brute force[23]. Government is the flashbang grenade that explodes in a crib, burning a hole in a toddler's chest in Georgia[24]. Government is a pair of fists that punches a homeless schizophrenic man to death in Fullerton, California[25]. Government is the arm that restrains a man who repeatedly begs to be left alone, ignores his pleas of "I can't breathe," and leaves him handcuffed on the ground to die[26]. Government is the sex offender that performs illegal anal cavity searches on men on the roadside[27]. Government is the SWAT team that uses environmental regulations as a pretext to raid a guitar factory where people earn an honest living[28].

The abuse and erosion of the US Constitution is too long to list. Just about every protection explicitly listed in the Bill of Rights has been violated. America's finest (and satirical) news source, *The Onion*, featured an article titled "Third Amendment Rights Group Celebrates Another Successful Year" in 2007[29]. Unfortunately, even the Third Amendment has been violated by the police (technically not the military, but a Select Militia nevertheless) who have taken over people's homes on at least one occasion, trying to gain a "tactical advantage" over their neighbors' homes where a crime was actually happening[30]. The National Guard's response during the Hurricane Katrina crisis in 2005 may also have included several Third Amendment violations[31].

The government, which is supposed to be the servant of the people, has turned into the boss. The president, who really should be the country's head butler, is instead treated like a king seated at the dining table while the masses are expected to offer him obsequious service.

Notes

1. Bridis, Ted. "Obama administration sets new record for withholding FOIA requests." *PBS* Newshour. 18 Mar. 2015. Web. <http://www.pbs.org/newshour/rundown/obama-administration-sets-new-record-withholding-foia-requests/>.

2. Mangu-Ward. Katherine. "Most Transparent Administration in History Releases Completely Redacted Document About Text Snooping." *Reason.com*. 13 May 2013. Web. <http://reason.com/blog/2013/05/13/most-transparent-administration-in-histo>.

3. Peterson, Andrea. "LOVEINT: When NSA officers use their spying power on love interests." *The Washington Post*. 24 Aug. 2013. Web. <https://www.washingtonpost.com/news/the-switch/wp/2013/08/24/loveint-when-nsa-officers-use-their-spying-power-on-love-interests/>.

4. Chaddock, Gail Russell. "Playing the IRS card: Six presidents who used the IRS to bash political foes." *The Christian Science Monitor*. 17 May 2013. Web. <http://www.csmonitor.com/USA/Politics/DC-Decoder/2013/0517/Playing-the-IRS-card-Six-presidents-who-used-the-IRS-to-bash-political-foes/President-Calvin-Coolidge-R>.

5. "Clerk charged with unlawful search of Joe the Plumber." *NBC24*. 28 Oct. 2008. Web. <http://nbc24.com/news/local/clerk-charged-with-unlawful-search-of-joe-the-plumber?id=213580>.

6. "Database plumbed about 'Joe.'" *The Washington Times*. 26 Oct. 2008. Web. <http://www.washingtontimes.com/news/2008/oct/26/database-plumbed-about-joe/>.

7. Hershey, William. "Jones-Kelley regrets allowing database searches." *Dayton Daily News*. 20 Nov. 2008. Web. <http://web.archive.org/web/20090125085056/http://www.western-star.com/n/content/oh/story/news/local/2008/11/20/ddn112008helenweb.html>.

8. Lussenhop, Jessica. "Is Anne Marie Rasmusson too hot to have a driver's license?" *City Pages.com*. 22 Feb. 2012. Web. <http://www.citypages.com/news/is-anne-marie-rasmusson-too-hot-to-have-a-drivers-license-6755567>.

9. Levine, Mike and Jack Date. "22 Million Affected by OPM Hack, Officials Say." *ABC News*. 9 Jul. 2015. Web. <http://abcnews.go.com/US/exclusive-25-million-affected-opm-hack-sources/story?id=32332731>.

10. Koren, Marina. "About Those Fingerprints Stolen in the OPM Hack." *The Atlantic*. 23 Sept. 2015. Web. <http://www.theatlantic.com/technology/archive/2015/09/opm-hack-fingerprints/406900/>.

11. Weise, Elizabeth. "IRS hack far larger than first thought." *USA Today*. 18 Aug. 2015. Web. <http://www.usatoday.com/story/tech/2015/08/17/irs-hack-get-transcript/31864171/>.

12. Greenberg, Andy. "Hackers Hit the IRS and Make Off With 100K Taxpayers' Files." *Wired*. 26 May 2015. Web. <https://www.wired.com/2015/05/hackers-hit-irs-access-100000-taxpayers-files/>.

13. Maas, K.C. and Josh Levs. "Newspaper sparks outrage for publishing names, addresses of gun permit holders." *CNN*. 27 Dec. 2012. Web. <http://www.cnn.com/2012/12/25/us/new-york-gun-permit-map/>.

14. Campbell, Colin. "Journal News Takes Down Controversial Map of Gun Owners." *Observer*. 18 Jan. 2013. Web. <http://observer.com/2013/01/journal-news-takes-down-controversial-map-of-gun-owners/>.

15. First National City Bank. "Hong Kong—A Success Story." *Foundation for Economic Education*. 1 Mar. 1960. Web. <https://fee.org/articles/hong-kong-a-success-story/>.

16. Peterson, Robert A. "Lessons in Liberty: Hong Kong, Crown Jewel of Capitalism." *Foundation for Economic Education*. 1 Jan. 1990. Web. <https://fee.org/articles/lessons-in-liberty-hong-kong-crown-jewel-of-capitalism/>.

17. Dikötter, Frank. *Mao's Great Famine*: The History of

China's Most Devastating Catastrophe, 1958-1962. New York: Bloomsbury, 2011. Print.

18. Jianying, Zha. "China: Surviving the Camps." *The New York Review of Books*. 16 Jan. 2016. Web. <http://www.nybooks.com/daily/2016/01/26/china-surviving-camps-cultural-revolution-memoir/>.

19. BBC. "Quick guide: China's economic reform. *BBC*. 3 Nov. 2006. Web. <http://news.bbc.co.uk/2/hi/asia-pacific/5237748.stm>.

20. Li, David and Shan Li. "The Chinese Economy after Deng." *The Journal of the International Institute*. Vol. 4, Issue 3, Summer 1997. Web. <http://quod.lib.umich.edu/j/jii/4750978.0004.307/--chinese-economy-after-deng?rgn=main;view=fulltext>.

21. Vogel, Ezra. "The great stabilizer." *The Economist*. 22 Oct. 2011. Web. <http://www.economist.com/node/21533354>.

22. Herchenroeder, Karl. "Michael Bloomberg blocks footage of Aspen Institute appearance." *The Aspen Times*. 13 Feb. 2015. Web. <http://www.aspentimes.com/news/15037917-113/michael-bloomberg-blocks-footage-of-aspen-institute-appearance>.

23. Quote often incorrectly attributed to President George Washington

24. Balko, Radley. "Georgia toddler critically injured by police's flash grenade." *The Washington Post*. 30 May 2014. Web. <https://www.washingtonpost.com/news/the-watch/wp/2014/05/30/georgia-toddler-critically-injured-by-polices-flash-grenade/?utm_term=.41f13b273e3d>.

25. Flaccus, Gillian. "Kelly Thomas killing: Police acquitted of death of homeless man in Calif." *The Christian Science Monitor*. 14 Jan. 2014. Web. <http://www.csmonitor.com/USA/Latest-News-Wires/2014/0114/Kelly-Thomas-killing-Police-acquitted-of-death-of-homeless-man-in-Calif>.

26. Eversley, Melanie and Mike James. "No charges in NYC chokehold death; federal inquiry launched." *USA Today*. 4 Dec. 2014. Web. <http://www.usatoday.com/story/news/nation/2014/12/03/chokehold-grand-jury/19804577/>.

27. Vielmetti, Bruce. "Ex-Milwaukee officer gets 26 months in prison for strip, cavity searches." *Milwaukee-Wisconsin Journal Sentinel*. 21 Jun. 2013. Web. <http://archive.jsonline.com/news/crime/ex-milwaukee-officer-gets-26-months-in-prison-for-strip-cavity-searches-b9938948z1-212486141.html>.

28. Jones, Susan. "After Two Raids, DOJ Decides No Criminal Charges Against Gibson Guitar Company." *CNSNews.com*. 7 Aug. 2012. Web. <http://cnsnews.com/news/article/after-two-raids-doj-decides-no-criminal-charges

-against-gibson-guitar-company>.

29. "Third Amendment Rights Group Celebrates Another Successful Year." *The Onion*. 5 Oct. 2007. Web. <http://www.theonion.com/article/third-amendment-rights-group-celebrates-another-su-2296>.

30. Somin, Ilya. "Federal court rejects Third Amendment claim against police officers." *The Washington Post*. 23 Mar. 2015. Web. <https://www.washingtonpost.com/news/volokh-conspiracy/wp/2015/03/23/federal-court-rejects-third-amendment-claim-against-police-officers/?utm_term=.b057c574784a>.

31. Rogers, James P. "Third Amendment Protections in Domestic Disasters." *Cornell Journal of Law and Public Policy*. Vol. 17:747. Web. <http://www.lawschool.cornell.edu/research/JLPP/upload/Rogers.pdf>.

Assault and Definition

Greg Camp

The military doctrine of the early twentieth century was that an ordinary soldier needed to be able to take aimed shots at targets out to a thousand yards one at a time. This was a change from previous centuries, exemplified by the battles of the Napoleonic Wars in which opposing battle lines would face each other and fire smooth-bored muskets for shot after shot in a drilled rhythm until one side abandoned the field.

In the second half of the nineteenth century, the invention of smokeless powder and self-contained cartridges allowed for much higher velocity rounds fired from a rifled barrel. The first example of this was the 8mm Lebel cartridge, developed by the French in 1886. The effective range of an infantryman opened out as the standard long arm issued to him became the bolt-action battle rifle. The best examples of these include the German Mauser 98, the British Short Model Lee Enfield, and the American Springfield 1903, a modified plagiarism of the Mauser. Another rifle that many American gun collectors will be familiar with is the Russian Mosin-Nagant, a weapon introduced in 1891 that remained in service through the Second World War and beyond.

These rifles fulfilled the role they were intended to play, but they are all long and heavy and fire full-power cartridges. There is a saying about the long arms of the Western allies, namely that the Germans went to war with the best hunting rifle, the Americans went with the best target rifle, and the British went with the best battle rifle. The Mauser action is a strong design, capable of handling high-pressure rounds and used to this day in hunting guns. As mentioned, the Springfield took the design of the Mauser bolt and added improved sights in keeping with the U.S. Army's emphasis on accuracy. The SMLE had a ten-round detachable box magazine, in contrast to the internal magazines of the others, and a slick action that allowed the Mad Minute, a shooting evaluation that required at least fifteen aimed shots at three hundred yards in sixty seconds. The record for this challenge was thirty-six hits.

The rate of fire possible with a bolt-action rifle is good enough in trench warfare or other static engagements. Such weapons can also work in battles that cover a lot of ground in a hurry, as the Germans demonstrated by using a shortened version of their Mauser in the blitzkrieg fighting of W.W. II. But even during the First World War, military theorists perceived a need for a primary arm of the infantryman that could send a lot of lead down range more rapidly. The Germans, French, and Russians experimented with submachine guns—weapons that are the size of a carbine, a shortened rifle, and fire a pistol cartridge. The United States came to this game too late, since the Thompson, called the Chicago typewriter during the gangster days of the twenties, was still having the bugs worked out when the war ended. The goal of the Thompson was to act as a "trench broom," sweeping out enemy soldiers with a high volume of fire. The French and the Russians also tried weapons that used a more powerful cartridge, intermediate between pistol rounds and those used by battle rifles, but design problems and the fortunes of war meant that these did not bear much fruit at the time.

But when the Second World War on the Eastern Front turned into a bitter slog, the Germans determined that a carbine using intermediate-power rounds and offering a high rate of fire, along with a detachable magazine to make reloading easier in a hurry would be a useful tool for fighting meter by meter against the waves of the Soviet Army. The weapon they came up with was the MP 44—the machine pistol of year 1944. It was called a machine pistol because some authority in the chain of command had ordered designers to stop proposing automatic rifles. When Hitler was presented with the new long arm, he is supposed to have labeled it the Sturmgewehr 44, *sturm* being the German for storm or assault, and *gewehr* meaning rifle. Hitler had a fondness for attaching "assault" to a wide assortment of people and things, presumably on propaganda grounds.

The StG 44 is the definitive example of the category of firearms called assault rifles in that it brought together all the necessary characteristics:

1. select fire capability
2. intermediate-power cartridge
3. detachable box magazine
4. effective range of 300 meters

The intermediate cartridge has already been explained. Select fire means that the rifle can fire in both semiautomatic mode—one shot for each squeeze of the trigger—or in fully automatic mode—fires as long as the trigger is squeezed either until released or the magazine goes empty. The effective range was accepted as much shorter than the more powerful battle rifles because of the mobile nature of fighting that became the norm as World War II was drawing to a close. Three hundred meters was more than enough in street-by-street combat.

Anyone taking a look at the StG 44 could not help but notice how many similarities there are with the most famous—or infamous—assault rifle, the AK-47, the Avtomat Kalashnikova (Kalashnikov's automatic rifle) of the year 1947. The Soviet weapon was influenced by the German, though the AK-47 has a different internal mechanism, but the essential characteristics are the same.

Just as the Communist nations got an assault rifle, so did America and its allies, the M-16, based on the AR-15, the Model 15 of ArmaLite, a small arms manufacturer. Its designer, Eugene Stoner, got his start in the aircraft industry, and his carbine design uses polymers and aluminum to reduce weight, along with an innovative system for cycling the action that will raise a fury of argument by supporters and detractors that need not trouble us here.

As should be expected, over the years since these three classic assault rifles were developed, many more models by many manufacturers have been designed. But without the characteristics of select-fire capability, using intermediate cartridges fed from a detachable box magazine, the weapon is not properly speaking an assault rifle.

And here we get into the weeds of the gun control debate. The Violence Policy Center, an anti-rights organization under the leadership of Josh Sugarmann, wrote a policy paper in 1988, titled, "Assault Weapons and Accessories in America," discussing how classes of firearms could be banned. In this document, the following statement makes clear the methodology of anti-rights advocates:

> Although handguns claim more than 20,000 lives a year, the issue of handgun restriction consistently remains a non-issue with the vast majority of legislators, the press, and public. The reasons for this vary: the power of the gun lobby; the tendency of both sides of the issue to resort to sloganeering and pre-packaged arguments when discussing the issue; the fact that until an individual is affected by handgun violence he or she is unlikely to work for handgun restrictions; the view that handgun violence is an "unsolvable" problem; the inability of the handgun restriction movement to organize itself into an effective electoral threat; and the fact that until someone famous is shot, or something truly horrible happens, handgun restriction is simply not viewed as a priority.

Assault weapons—just like armor-piercing bullets, machine guns, and plastic firearms—are a new topic. **The weapons' menacing looks, coupled with the public's confusion over fully automatic machine guns versus semi-automatic assault weapons—anything that looks like a machine gun is assumed to be a machine gun—can only increase the chance of public support for restrictions on these weapons.** In addition, few people can envision a practical use for these weapons[1]. (Emphasis added.)

This is likely the origin of the phrase, assault weapons. It is an effort to obfuscate classes of firearms with a goal to ban as many as possible.

Outright falsehoods are easy to knock down with evidence, but the VPC's policy paper shows confusions that too many have over what makes an assault rifle. As mentioned above, one key characteristic is the select-fire capability. If you can only get one bullet expended for each squeeze of the trigger, you do not have a fully automatic weapon. We have to recognize that "automatic," unfortunately, has gone through a transition over the twentieth century. In the late nineteenth century, firearms were developed that today we call "self-loading," meaning that with each trigger squeeze, the action cycles, loading a new cartridge into the chamber. That was called "automatic." Another name is "semiautomatic," the term typically used among the gun community now. "Automatic" at present generally means continual firing as long as the trigger is squeezed and the magazine has ammunition. (Recall here Justice Stevens's ambiguous usage of "automatic" with regard to firearms[2].)

But the so-called assault rifles sold brand-new to the public in the United States are all semiautomatic. That goes for the AR-15, for the AK-47 variants, and for every other rifle that does not require manual cycling by the user. Calling these guns "assault rifles" is done either out of deceptiveness or ignorance. "Assault weapon" is even worse, since as the VPC admits elsewhere in the document cited, the term has no exact definition. This leaves it available to anyone who wants to define it any old way, typically for the purpose of building support for bans.

The claim that "few people can envision a practical use for these weapons" is equally slippery, since it is hard to verify in what it literally says without careful surveying that avoids biased questions, but we can consider if there are practical uses for the many semiautomatic rifles today. And here we have good answers.

Despite claims made by gun control advocates, such rifles are used by hunters. That includes deer hunters, but it is especially true for people seeking to control the feral hog populations that damage farmland and wilderness areas of the southern U.S.[3] These animals are not native to the region and have been destructive since their introduction in the early days of European exploration of this continent. In Arkansas, for example, no license is required, and no bag limit is imposed on the hunting of hogs in recognition of the need to remove them from the environment. And here is a case in which the semiautomatic rifle with a detachable magazine is the best tool for the job. Unlike deer, hogs are tough animals that are quick moving. Contrary to the belief that needing many rounds is a sign of a poor hunter, in the case of feral pigs, the job often does require more than one shot. These rifles are also popular in competition shooting. The AR-15, for example, has considerable potential as the basis of a target rifle, thanks to its design.

And then there is the thorny question of self-defense. Hollywood to the contrary, handguns are compromise weapons. Their power is low, both due to cartridge capacity and barrel length, meaning that the one-shot stop of an attacker is much more common in film than real life. We carry handguns because they are convenient for concealment. They can be used for self-defense, but this takes learning the skill. Semiautomatic rifles are easier to learn and easier to use effectively. The greater power produces a more reliable stop of someone threatening your life, and the longer sight radius—distance between the rear sight and front sight—aids in aiming.

The history of the assault rifle is fascinating and detailed, and the arguments offered by advocates of gun control depend on people being ignorant of the facts. One point of this book is to clear up confusion, to show the reality of guns and gun rights. The case made against "assault weapons," upon examination falls apart, leaving us to recognize, as the VPC showed, that the ultimate goal is the removal of all legally owned firearms, regardless of design. But when the case for gun control is based on errors and deceptions, the argument for gun rights is made that much the stronger.

Notes

1. "Conclusion." *Assault Weapons and Accessories in America. Violence Policy Center*. 1988. Web. <http://www.vpc.org/publications/assault-weapons-and-accessories-in-america/assault-weapons-and-accessories-in-america-conclusion/>.

2. See pages 31 - 32.

3. Mississippi State University Extension. "Damage by Pigs." *Wild Pig Info*. 19 May 2014. Web. <http://wildpiginfo.msstate.edu/damage-caused-by-pigs.html>.

Do SOMETHING, please!

Ranjit Singh

Every mass shooting in the United States is followed rapidly by comments from elitist politicians and opinion makers about how we never do anything and demands that we should "Do Something." President Obama even started a Twitter hashtag—#DoSomething—following the Umpqua Community College shooting.[1]

The one something that can actually make a difference—allowing vulnerable people to defend themselves easily and quickly by using reactive, proportional force—is *always* off the table. The natural right of self-defense is effectively usurped. Instead, the proposals made in the quest to "Do Something" are often akin to running ten laps around a burning building in order to put out the fire.

Each One, Teach One

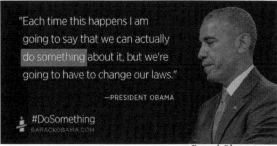

BarackObama.com

Associated Press

A government consisting of a formidable alphabet soup of multi-billion dollar agencies like the DEA, FBI, and the NSA is unable to keep marijuana and other "controlled" substances away from high school kids. How on earth is such a government ever going to keep guns out of the hands of calculating crooks who methodically plan their crimes and figure out ways of illegally getting a gun regardless of what the law says? Is a "gun-free zone" sign listing harsh federal penalties going to dissuade a suicidal mass murderer into leaving his weapons before entering a school or a building? As reported in *The Real Revo.com*, the July 2015 ISIS-inspired terrorist attack on U.S. military installations in Chattanooga, TN, is a damning indictment of the idiocy of gun-free zones[2].

The government's armed agents are not omniscient, omnipotent gods—nor do we want them to be. They cannot be present everywhere, and cannot be available at all times. Often times, the government's armed agents show up to send a dead body for an autopsy, instead of saving a living person. The police *do not* even have a duty to protect the people. There are various court cases that have asserted this conclusion[3]. (See *Warren v District of Columbia* for a stomach-churning example[4].) Is it willful malevolence or inordinate stupidity on the part of hoplophobes to expect those agents to defend us?

The mad rush to "Do Something" is best seen in New York's SAFE Act. This appalling law, which was passed with minimal discussion about three weeks after the Newtown massacre, is surpassed in its haste only by its stupidity. Under the guise of necessity, it was passed in the middle of the night, bypassing a required three-day review period[5]. New York legislators, in all their wisdom, spent more time in a nonsensical, trivial debate on making yogurt the official state snack the following year than on a law that imposed a burden on a fundamental human right[6]. The haste with which the NY SAFE Act was passed accidentally led to even the police being subjected to these rules; an exemption for current and retired law enforcement was only added as an afterthought[7]. Why some citizens such as current and retired law enforcement officers are "more equal" than other citizens still remains an unanswered question.

The NY SAFE Act had a lot of "Do Something" provisions such as banning magazines that could hold over ten rounds, requiring law-abiding citizens, who pose the least amount of risk to society, to put no more than seven rounds in a ten-round magazine—that was thrown out by the courts—requiring an unworkable background check for ammunition purchases —which was later indefinitely suspended—and mandating "safe storage" of firearms. It also expanded the definition of so-called assault weapons, created a registry of such weapons, and required mental health professionals to report credible threats of violence to the state government, which would in theory allow the state to confiscate a patient's weapons[8].

Not *one* of these "Do Something" provisions is going to stop the next massacre. A crook or a suicidal lunatic bent on killing his fellow human beings is not going to give a hoot about any of these laws and will figure out a way of illegally obtaining a weapon and ammunition. A crook is not going to worry about safe storage laws or about a law that says he cannot own a fifteen-round magazine or that he can only load seven rounds. And most importantly, a crook, who has a good chance of already being a convicted felon, will *never* subject himself to a background check or register his weapons with the police.

NY SAFE Act-style gun registration is no magical vaccine against violence. Even if every gun belonging to every citizen is registered, it is not going to inoculate an individual from aggressive violence. To top it off, mental health professionals simply cannot predict violence. They don't possess a sixth sense like the "precogs" in the movie, *Minority Report*. In all likelihood, New York State will get a lot of false positives that will result in the abuse of the natural, civil rights of law-abiding patients. There is evidence that this is indeed happening[9]. Even if mental health professionals correctly identify and report threats, there is no guarantee that the state will act on those reports. Government bureaucracy has a miraculous way of producing failures even under the most favorable circumstances.

The sale of a handgun to Dylan Roof, the white supremacist who killed nine of his fellow human beings in Charleston, South Carolina, after sitting with them in an hour-long Bible study, is a case in point[10]. Roof had a criminal background, having been arrested on a drug charge, and should not have been able to purchase a gun. However, the FBI fumbled the check, first by contacting the wrong police department and then by not following up with the Lexington County prosecutor's office. The gun was legally sold to Roof after a waiting period of three business days[11]. This three-business-day period is now being called the "Charleston Loophole" by those demanding more gun control, including the Democratic Party's 2016 presidential nominee, Hillary Clinton[12]. After *a whole two months* since the sale, Roof used his gun to commit his heinous crime. During this gap, the Lexington County prosecutor's office never responded to the FBI, and the FBI dropped the matter.

As evident from the government's inaction, prolonging the "Charleston Loophole" period to even two months would not have resolved the underlying problem of government incompetence. As the old adage goes, justice delayed is justice denied. Likewise, delaying the exercise of rights is denying the exercise of rights. The kerfuffle over the "Charleston Loophole" is driven by gun controllers salivating at the ability to block gun sales through dilatory tactics by slowly extending the background check period until it is an indefinite, arbitrary waiting period.

When a massacre happens, logic is sacrificed to emotion, and the calls to "Do Something" lead to demands for the tightening of the grip by the boa constrictor hoplophobes. The prey, of course, is Liberty herself. The use of immediate, reactive, proportional violence by law-abiding citizens is put at risk, and mature adults, who are in no way inferior to the police, are infantilized, accorded the dubious privilege of becoming unarmed victims. Politicians give emotional, tear-ridden speeches about the scourge of "gun" violence, using victims' families as props to pass more ineffective laws, while ignoring the one solution that will lower the body count. Progressives bash "uncivilized" America while fantasizing about importing civilization from the "enlightened" continent of Europe. And meanwhile, people who would much rather be armed, alive, and unknown, are disarmed, dead, and memorialized only by having ineffective laws named after them.

In the midst of all this, gun control advocates ignore the very real possibility of the abuse of power by government officials and demand that citizens trust them with a monopoly of guns. In the bid to move toward a government monopoly of guns, stories like the rape of a New York City school teacher by gun-toting, drunk policeman Michael Pena[13] will be brushed aside. Stories like the assault of a female bartender by Chicago policeman Anthony Abbate[14] and his department's attempts to cover up the crime[15] will be swept under the rug. Stories like the shooting of Akai

Gurley, during the immediate aftermath of which the New York City policeman involved allegedly texted his union representative instead of calling for help[16], will be ignored. Tragedies like the Danziger Bridge shooting in the aftermath of Hurricane Katrina, in which New Orleans police shot six innocent people, two of whom died, won't be considered[17]. Stories of official lying, such as the fabricated DUI citations handed out by Utah policewoman Lisa Steed[18], will be disregarded. Historically important examples, such as South Korean policeman Woo Bum-kon's 1982 killing of fifty-six people[19], or Belgian Congolese constable William Unek's 1957 killing of 32 people[20], will be sent down the memory-hole. Progressive hoplophobes will continue their naive, pig-headed, perverse "Trust Government" logic and demand bigger, muscular government despite ample evidence of the danger involved in doing so. Those who are wary of ever-increasing government power will be denigrated as naysayers, bitter clingers, paranoid whackjobs, and gun humpers.

In addition to ignoring the abuse of power, hoplophobes will also ignore the incompetence of government officials. Stories like that of DEA agent Lee Paige[21], who shot himself in the foot in front a classroom full of kids after haughtily saying, "I'm the only one in this room professional enough that I know of to carry this Glock .40" will be ignored. The shooting of innocent bystanders in Manhattan by police trying to subdue an emotionally disturbed man and then charging that man with the shooting will be set aside[22]. Hoplophobes will tell the people that they cannot be trusted with guns, but the police, who are no different from ordinary people, can be trusted because they are "trained," wear neatly-pressed uniforms, and carry a shiny badge.

When brushing aside government malevolence and incompetence in pursuit of rights restrictions, progressive hoplophobes will ignore the possibility of willful dereliction of duty. Stories like that of Sheriff's Deputy Yvan Fernandez of Lee County, FL, who ignored a dying woman's 911 call so he could finish eating his pizza, will be swept under the rug[23]. Alarming real-life precedents like that of Miami-Dade police officer Dario Socarras, who was filmed kissing and spending time with his girlfriend while ignoring calls for armed robbery and burglary, and filmed drinking coffee for nine whole minutes while ignoring a call to check on an unconscious five-month old baby, will be disregarded[24]. Tragic stories like that of nine-year old Omaree Varela, whose death at the hands of his own mother could have been prevented had the police done their duty and listened to a 911 call recording, will be ignored for the sake of expedience in pursuit of a gun control agenda[25]. Yet progressive hoplophobes will tell the people to trust the government and sacrifice their own safety in order to lasso a mythical common-good unicorn.

Irrational calls for hobbling the Second Amendment by passing more laws to harass lawful citizens into giving up their firearms often come from hypocrites whose livelihoods depend on the First Amendment. The language of the First Amendment is reduced to lofty blather without the ability to use force, protected by the Second Amendment, to defend it. There is a reason Pastor Terry Jones and Pamela Gellar can criticize Islam in the open in America, but Lars Vilks and Kurt Westergaard have to hide in Europe.

Consider the case of journalist and former presidential speechwriter, David Frum, who worked for President George W. Bush. Frum, who identifies with the Republican Party, wrote an article in *The Atlantic*[26] after the Charleston church shooting advocating "greater safety through incremental steps" such as requiring *all* gun owners to get "liability" insurance (a private-sector-enforced gun tax by another name), and requiring "meaningful" training for carry-permit holders. In that article, Frum even whined about how florists in the state of Florida have to go through six weeks of courses at a cost of $600 to sell flowers, but carry permit applicants only have to submit a "certificate of competency" from a firearms instructor. (Why florists have to spend $600 and go through six weeks of training to get the government's permission to sell flowers is beyond me.)

Wouldn't it be swell if the same recommendations that Frum is making to constrain the Second Amendment were applied to the First Amendment, on which his journalistic profession depends? After all, people like David Frum were cheerleaders for the Iraq War, which cost America over 4,000 lives and $3 trillion. For the sake of protecting the country from speech writers' idiocy in pushing future wars, shouldn't we require people like Frum to "produce evidence of good conduct and mental stability"? What about liability insurance for speech writers like Frum's colleague Michael Gerson who do their part in goading the country to war by injecting unsubstantiated claims into a President's State of the Union speech[27]?

Why stop at liability insurance or training? Following David Frum's boa constrictor logic of "incremental steps," journalists and speech writers who acted as cheerleaders for a war based on faulty or fabricated WMD claims should perhaps be incrementally muzzled, so that they cannot fire off nonsense that drags America into yet another war in the Middle East.

The hypocrisy of some journalists who use the First Amendment to call for constraining the Second Amendment is in a class of its own. Any "incremental steps" for the purpose of "greater safety" is best translated as the incremental choking of Liberty.

The media has a tremendous bias against guns. It sensationalizes the usage of guns in crime while brushing aside crime committed with other weapons. Even with a single crime spree, the usage of a firearm receives greater publicity. The 2014 Isla Vista massacre had three stabbing victims, and three shooting victims. The massacre was publicized and is remembered as a gun attack, instead of a knife, vehicle, and gun attack. Google's search engine suggests "shooting" as the third word if you use "Isla Vista" as the first two words, not "killings" or "massacre."

On the extreme end of the incremental "Do Something!" spectrum is the "Do Everything!" crowd, who believe that a complete ban on firearms will somehow end the majority of, if not all human violence. My ancestral country India should be a dreamland for the gun ban crowd, given how strictly firearms are restricted there. Yet massacres and homicides attributed to political and non-political causes happen there on a regular basis. Violent criminals in the largely non-violent land of Gandhi have a preference for tridents, spears, knives, swords, daggers, crowbars, hammers, ropes, and kerosene when it comes to tools of their trade. India also has an (obviously) illegal cottage industry that manufactures *kattas*, or country-made handguns. And with the advent, export, and rapid democratization of modern technology around the world, it is not hard to imagine 3D-printed guns in India in the future. No law or regulation will prevent criminals and terrorists from obtaining the weaponry they want to slaughter law-abiding people who are *intentionally made defenseless and dependent* by their governments.

Notes

1. Obama, Barack (@BarackObama). "Retweet if you agree: It's time for Congress to put politics aside and #DoSomething about gun violence." 8 Oct. 2015, 11:16 AM. Tweet.

2. Walker, R.D. "Marines Down in Chattanooga." *The Real REVO.com*. 16 Jul. 2015. Web. <http://therealrevo.com/blog/?p=133742>.

3. Kasler, Peter. "Police Have No Duty To Protect Individuals." *Firearms and Liberty.com*. 1992. Web. <https://www.firearmsandliberty.com/kasler-protection.html>.

4. Warren, et al. v. District of Columbia, et al. 444 A.2d 1. District of Columbia Court of Appeals. 1981. *Google Scholar*. Web. <https://scholar.google.com/scholar_case?case=9108468254125174344&q=warren-v-district-of-columbia&hl=en&as_sdt=2006>.

5. Breidenbach, Michelle. "The Safe Act 'emergency': How Cuomo, past governors bypassed public to make laws." *Syracuse.com*. 13 Mar. 2013. Web. <http://www.syracuse.com/news/index.ssf/2013/03/state_emergency_gun_law.html>.

6. Weaver, Teri. "NY Safe Act or yogurt: Which was debated

longer on state Senate floor?" *Syracuse.com*. 7 May 2014. Web. <http://www.syracuse.com/news/index.ssf/2014/05/ny_safe_act_or_yogurt_which_got_more_debate_time_in_state_senate.html>.

7. Sullum, Jacob. "Cops Are Outraged That New York's New Magazine Limit Could Apply to Them." *Reason.com*. 18 Jan. 2013. Web. <http://reason.com/blog/2013/01/18/cops-are-outraged-that-new-yorks-new-mag>.

8. Sullum, Jacob. "State Police Struggle to Understand New York's Crazy New Gun Law." *Reason.com*. 11 Oct. 2013. Web. <http://reason.com/blog/2013/10/11/state-police-struggle-to-understand-new>.

9. Sullum, Jacob. "If You Want to Keep Your Guns in New York, Avoid Mental Health Professionals." *Reason.com*. 20 Oct. 2014. Web. <http://reason.com/blog/2014/10/20/if-you-want-to-keep-your-guns-in-new-yor>.

10. Brumfield, Ben and Martin Savidge. "Funerals begin in Charleston shootings; one victim called 'symbol of love.'" *CNN*. 26 Jun. 2015. Web. <http://edition.cnn.com/2015/06/25/us/charleston-church-shooting-main/>.

11. Schmidt, Michael S. "Background Check Flaw Let Dylann Roof Buy Gun, F.B.I. Says." *The New York Times*. 10 Jul. 2015. Web. <http://www.nytimes.com/2015/07/11/us/background-check-flaw-let-dylann-roof-buy-gun-fbi-says.html>.

12. Clorclari, Corey. "How a little-known loophole allowed the Charleston shooter to get a gun: More people need to know about this." *HillaryClinton.com*. 30 Nov. 2015. Web. <https://www.hillaryclinton.com/feed/how-loophole-youve-never-heard-allowed-charleston-shooter-buy-his-gun/>.

13. Gregorian, Dareh. "Judge denies rape cop Michael Pena's bid for reduced sentence in 2011 sex attack of elementary school teacher." *New York Daily News*. 26 Mar. 2015. Web. <https://www.nydailynews.com/new-york/nyc-crime/judge-nixes-rape-michael-pena-bid-reduced-sentence-article-1.2163367>.

14. Sweeney, Annie and Jason Meisner. "Jury finds in favor of bartender in cop bar beating case, 'Justice was served.'" *Chicago Tribune*. 14 Nov. 2012. Web. <http://articles.chicagotribune.com/2012-11-14/news/chi-verdict-reached-in-cop-bar-beating-case-20121113_1_code-of-silence-policy-karolina-obrycka-chicago-cop-anthony-abbate>.

15. Sweeney, Annie and Jason Meisner. "Police cover-up found in bartender beating: Jury rules against police, awards $850,000 in case brought to light by brutal video." *Chicago Tribune*. 14 Nov. 2012. Web. <http://articles.chicagotribune.com/2012-11-14/news/ct-met-abbate-verdict-20121114_1_karolina-obrycka-officer-anthony-abbate-jury-rules>.

16. Parascandola, Rocco and Oren Yaniv. "EXCLUSIVE: Rookie

NYPD officer who shot Akai Gurley in Brooklyn stairwell was texting union rep as victim lay dying." *New York Daily News*. 5 Dec. 2014. Web. <https://www.nydailynews.com/new-york/brooklyn/exclusive-texted-union-rep-akai-gurley-lay-dying-article-1.2034219>.

17. NPR Staff. "'Shots On The Bridge' Unpacks A Tangled Story Of Deceit And Tragedy." *NPR*. 18 Aug. 2015. Web. <http://www.npr.org/2015/08/18/432570962/shots-on-the-bridge-unpacks-a-tangled-story-of-deceit-and-tragedy>.

18. Green-Miner, Brittany and Todd Tanner. "Lawsuit filed by alleged false DUI victims of Steed." *Fox13Now.com*. 14 Dec. 2012. Web. <http://fox13now.com/2012/12/14/lawsuit-filed-by-alleged-false-dui-victims-of-steed/>.

19. "Crime history - Korean cop kills 57 people during 8-hour rampage." *Washington Examiner*. 23 Apr. 2009. Web. <http://www.washingtonexaminer.com/crime-history-korean-cop-kills-57-people-during-8-hour-rampage/article/100378>.

20. Unek, William. "Constable Runs Amok in Africa, Kills 32." *Corpus Christi Times*. 14 Feb. 1957: 32. Print.

21. Alvarez, Alex. "DEA Agent Is Suing Government For Allegedly Releasing Video Of Him Shooting Himself In The Foot." *Mediaite.com*. 1 Feb. 2011. Web. <http://www.mediaite.com/online/dea-agent-is-suing-government-for-allegedly-releasing-video-of-him-

shooting-himself-in-the-foot/>.

22. McKinley, Jr., James C. "Unarmed Man Is Charged With Wounding Bystanders Shot by Police Near Times Square." *The New York Times*. 4 Dec. 2013. Web. <http://www.nytimes.com/2013/12/05/nyregion/unarmed-man-is-charged-with-wounding-bystanders-shot-by-police-near-times-square.html?_r=1>.

23. Boggioni, Tom. "Florida deputy fired for ignoring 911 call from dying woman so he could finish his pizza." *Raw Story.com*. 24 Apr. 2015. Web. <http://www.rawstory.com/2015/04/florida-deputy-fired-for-ignoring-911-call-from-dying-woman-so-he-could-finish-his-pizza/>.

24. "Miami-Dade Police Kendall Squad Caught Ignoring Emergency Calls, Shopping On Camera (Video)." *The Huffington Post*. 7 Apr. 2013. Web. <http://www.huffingtonpost.com/2013/02/05/miami-dade-police-squad-caught-kendall_n_2621924.html>.

25. Laffin, Nancy. "Dispatcher upset by officers' inaction at Omaree 911 call." *KOAT.com*. 7 Feb. 2014. Web. <http://www.koat.com/target7/dispatcher-upset-by-officers-inaction-at-omaree-911-call/24360022>.

26. Frum, David. "Mass Shootings Are Preventable." *The Atlantic*. 23 Jun. 2015. Web. <http://www.theatlantic.com/politics/archive/2015/06/mass-shootings-are-preventable/396644/>.

27. "Profile: Michael Gerson." *History Commons.org*. Web. <http://historycommons.org/entity.jsp?entity=michael_gerson>.

Part IV: Knowledge destroys Ignorance, Familiarity destroys Fear

Use It or Lose It

Ranjit Singh

Countries that do not have strong protections for the freedom of speech routinely go through atrocious restrictions on that right. The public in these countries is *habituated* to the restrictions and responds with a collective shrug when such infringements happen.

My country of origin, India, is a notorious case in point. The government routinely bans books, videos, and movies that it considers "unacceptable." India abandoned her very own gifted son, Salman Rushdie, and banned his book, *The Satanic Verses*, because *some* Muslims found the book offensive and considered it blasphemous.

Germany bans Nazi memorabilia and signage. France banned all conspicuous religious insignia in its government schools in 2004. China continues to harass artist Ai Weiwei for daring to mock the Communist Party. Many countries routinely censor the press, or influence the reporting of news. In today's Internet-driven world, this includes blocking search engines, search terms, and web sites. The most famous example of this is the Great Firewall of China. Some countries run their own propaganda mouthpieces. *Pravda, IRNA, Xinhua*—the list is long. Before India's economy underwent market reforms in the 1990s, there was only one TV station, operated by the government. The Ministry of Truth described in George Orwell's *1984* exists in the real world.

Few people in the countries mentioned above demand complete freedom of expression. The people have been made accustomed to the idea that freedom is something that is allowed by the government. They are not used to the idea that freedom is theirs and theirs alone and the government must not tread on it.

In contrast to the above, America, true to its exceptional nature, has a solid foundation for the freedom of speech. Here, the ACLU successfully defended the right of loathsome neo-Nazis of the National Socialist Party of America to march through a neighborhood of Jewish holocaust survivors in the Village of Skokie, Illinois in 1977. Here, Christians can freely wear large crosses, Muslim girls can wear hijabs, Jewish boys can wear their yarmulkes, and Sikh boys can wear their turbans in government schools. Here, people like Kanye West can claim that President George W. Bush doesn't care about black people, Stephen Colbert and Jon Stewart can mercilessly mock the Republican Party, and Rush Limbaugh can offensively and disgustingly call President Barack Obama a "Halfrican American" without getting harassed by the government. And unlike pre-1991 socialist India's government monopoly TV station, Doordarshan, America has a raucous multitude of media outlets, PBS and NPR notwithstanding.

The fundamental human right to speech in America is protected from infringement by the Bill of Rights, and the people are used to this glorious tradition. Any attempt to infringe on this right is met with strong opposition.

Americans routinely use this right and would never give it up or accept limitations, despite the fact that some people abuse it. This routine use has perpetuated a *culture of free speech* which will hopefully live on forever. If the exercise of this right becomes limited out of fear (as is the case with media self-censorship with Mohammed cartoons), or is abridged for the sake of politics (as is the case with calls for a constitutional amendment to overturn the *Citizens United* judgment), this right will eventually wear out and cease to exist.

Use it or lose it. It's that simple. This principle also applies to the right to keep and bear arms. One of the crucial aspects of American exceptionalism is found in the tradition of firearms ownership that new immigrants like me often find shocking and incomprehensible. Foreign governments rarely respect this freedom of their people, and the people are *habituated* to this culture. It is not just immigrants like me who find gun ownership shocking and alien. Native-born Americans who come from families that do not own weapons or live in subcultures that are averse to their presence, unsurprisingly react the same way that new immigrants would.

In the long term, if the right to arms is to be protected, the exercise of this right should be widespread. It should not be limited to rural Iowa or the Colorado countryside or Wyoming. The greater the firearms exposure that the law-abiding, sane, residents of New York City, Boston, San Francisco, and other "liberal" cities get, the more the right to arms will be used. And the more this right is used, the less the likelihood of it being lost.

It is not hard to imagine a future where the ownership of and familiarity with firearms dwindles so much that the Second Amendment is repealed using the prescribed constitutional process or effectively bled to death through a thousand regulatory cuts. This would be extremely dangerous and reduce the people to sheep who, without the ability to assert their rights with might, can be corralled in whichever way the government desires.

Might is unfortunately often right, and rights won't exist when the people lose their armed might. The First Amendment protects the right of people—acting individually or in groups—to free speech. There are already emotional calls for a constitutional convention to overturn the *Citizens United* judgment by restricting the First Amendment to groups of people acting together strictly as a media corporation and to allow the government to dictate what other groups of people can or cannot say. If this mad course of action is pursued, America, where you can walk into any library and easily find Salman Rushdie's reviled book, will turn into India, the UK, Germany, France, or China, where speech in all of its forms can be arbitrarily censored. The Left's myopic, hysterical demands that the government have the power to ban *Hillary: The Movie* will give the Right, when in office, the power to ban *Fahrenheit 9/11*. A country whose founders took enormous risks to publish pamphlets like *Common Sense* will lose its connection to its own history and will resemble the tyranny that it overthrew. After all, the British monarch in 1776 would have loved to ban *King George: The Pamphlet*.

The Demographic-Knowledge Threat to the Second Amendment

Ranjit Singh

Statistics show that the per capita gun ownership rate in the United States is more than one gun per citizen. America is the most heavily armed nation on the planet. This per capita number may seem reassuring to gun owners, but does not show the true discomforting picture. The number of American *households* that own guns is somewhere around 30-40%. This second statistic, which is the more important number, used to be a lot higher in the past - closer to 55-60% in 1970s, and has been going down over time[1,2,3,4]. And herein lies what I call the demographic-knowledge threat to the Second Amendment, which is a dangerous negative feedback loop involving gun ownership and gun rights.

The demographic aspect of the threat is purely one of strength in numbers. Even if there are a hundred guns for a hundred voters, if one voter owns all one hundred guns and the remaining ninety-nine voters don't own any, the majority can and *will* outvote the lone gun owner and take away her rights. This should be highly disconcerting because we live in a modern culture which is increasingly disrespectful of the Constitution, wherein individual rights are viewed as subordinate to the collective wishes of the majority mob. In this culture, government has grown while liberty has receded. While the government (expectedly) pushes the limits, bending and sometimes even breaking the law, the people are often distracted or uncaring. After all, the latest celebrity scandal is more interesting than some arcane constitutional debate. At the same time, those who are actually paying attention are often cheering the government when their favored party is in power and their own policy preferences are shoved down everyone else's throats at the expense of liberty and in violation of the Constitution.

The knowledge aspect of the threat is closely associated with the demographics of gun ownership. It is not about racial or ethnic statistics, but purely about knowledge and familiarity. Gun controllers have an unstated intention of decreasing the ownership of firearms among the people. *Their ideal gun ownership rate for American households is 0%, and the policies they push are meant to have that effect.* Gun controllers claim that their intention is to promote "gun safety" or "gun reform," but the policies that they promote have the effect of decreasing the percentage of people owning firearms. If they succeed, ignorance will increase in the long run. As ignorance increases, so will hoplophobia and apathy towards gun ownership. This will lead to demands for even more gun control, which will be met with a large collective apathetic shrug by non-gun owners[5], with small pockets of impassioned, yet futile, resistance from gun owners. As this negative feedback loop gains strength, more assaults on the natural human right to self-defense will be made, further decreasing gun ownership and increasing ignorance, in a continuous loop which will eventually take gun ownership to 0%.

Chances of preserving the Second Amendment for future generations depends on spreading knowledge and increasing the number of households owning firearms. Such an increase must be broad-based and diverse, covering urban, suburban, and rural households. Such an increase must cover everyone - immigrants and umpteenth-generation Americans, straight and gay, black, white, brown and yellow, Ph.D. recipients and high school dropouts. The increasing concentration of more guns in fewer hands must be reversed to include many more and non-traditional hands.

If this does not happen, in the long run, the gun controllers will win. The negative feedback loop, which is already underway, must be broken. Firearms education is the key, and if it is not the number one priority, the Second Amendment will slowly but surely erode and fall by the wayside.

Notes

1. Tavernise, Sabrina and Robert Gebeloff. "Share of Homes With Guns Shows 4-Decade Decline." *The New York Times*. 9 Mar. 2013. Web. <http://www.nytimes.com/2013/03/10/us/rate-of-gun-ownership-is-down-survey-shows.html?pagewanted=all&_r=0>.

2. Pew Research Center. "Why Own a Gun? Protection Is Now Top Reason: Perspectives of Gun Owners, Non-Owners." *People-Press.com*. 12 Mar. 2013. Web. <http://www.people-press.org/2013/03/12/section-3-gun-ownership-trends-and-demographics/>.

3. Gallup. "Guns." *Gallup.com*. 2016. Web. <http://www.gallup.com/poll/1645/guns.aspx>.

4. Bialik, Carl. "Gun Counts Can Be Hit-or-Miss." *The Wall Street Journal*. 22 Mar. 2013. Web. <http://www.wsj.com/articles/SB10001424127887324103504578374692383804654>.

5. Jones, Jeffrey M. "Public Believes Americans Have Right to Own Guns." *Gallup.com*. 27 Mar. 2008. Web. <http://www.gallup.com/poll/105721/Public-Believes-Americans-Right-Own-Guns.aspx>.

A New Evangelism

Ranjit Singh

There are multi-faceted threats to this basic American freedom, and the only thing that can protect our freedom in the long run is the elimination of ignorance. Knowledge is power. As an old Hindu prayer says, the light of knowledge destroys the darkness of ignorance. Familiarity destroys fear.

A broad-based awareness, possession, and regular use of firearms is the only thing that can guarantee that this right will not be removed from future generations.

Demystification is the cure for hoplophobia. When the average citizen who is unfamiliar with firearms learns them inside out, the misleading verbiage and statistical torture put out by gun controllers will be exposed in all their disgusting nudity. A general understanding of the right to arms as a natural right, unaffected by utilitarian nonsense, will help stop the gun controllers. I can assert this based on my own personal experience.

Gun rights groups are already engaged in training and education activities. However, there is a limit to what they can do. The biggest gains of education will come when gun owners individually and independently introduce people to arms. When 80 million gun owners introduce 80 million non-gun owners to firearms, the effect of it will be spectacular and unprecedented. Even if only one-third of the people who learn about firearms become gun owners, they will substantially swell the numerical strength of a group that will have something to lose with governmental infringement on their precious right. Those who have something to lose will fight for it, whereas those who don't will be indifferent to what they perceive as someone else's loss, without realizing that the loss is also theirs[1].

Where an invitation from an organization like the NRA has a good chance of repelling someone, direct human contact with another person can better help make the case for training. The media's methodical stereotyping and demonization of gun owners as uneducated, racist, overly religious, rural whites will fall apart when a non-gun owner encounters a normal fellow human being who knows firearms and can articulate his or her belief in the right to self-defense, thereby erasing the stereotypes pushed by the media.

As outlined earlier, people unfamiliar with firearms must be trained at large if the Second Amendment is to survive in the long run. However, there are some groups of people who will be an integral part of—to borrow a phrase from the eternally execrable Vladimir Lenin—the "commanding heights" of politics, the law, and popular culture, and must be a primary target for education and outreach efforts. These are law school students, journalism students, and creative arts students.

Today's law school students will be tomorrow's lawyers, judges, and politicians. Close to half the US Congress have law degrees. Judges, obviously, do as well. These are the people who will determine the future of the Second Amendment. It is essential that law school students be exposed to firearms if they do not have any prior exposure. This is the best way to decrease the incidence of hoplophobia in this important group. Law schools are the belly of the beast that is modern academia, and that is where the fight to preserve the Second Amendment must be taken.

Journalism students will become future opinion makers and should be another high-priority focus for firearms education and outreach efforts. Decreasing the incidence of hoplophobia among journalism students is the best way to decrease media bias in the long run. Just about every college newspaper I have read has revealed a bias among student-journalists and is a good predictor of what these student-journalists will do when they graduate and work for real-world media outlets. Student-journalists must absolutely be won over if the problem of media bias is to be ameliorated over the coming decades.

The creative arts group is another important group, because they will be future authors, poets, scriptwriters, and movie directors and will influence popular culture. This group must be included as a high priority for education and outreach.

None of this in any way means that college students outside of the above groups are unimportant. Exposing *all* law-abiding, sane college students is a must. Firearms education and exposure should ideally be done at a younger age, but if children in government schools are not given this opportunity, they can get it on their own volition as independent, responsible college-age adults.

The bottom line is that more groups of our fellow Americans need to be brought into our community, especially those who are not typically thought of as gun owners. The rights protected by the Second Amendment do not have to be lost to demographic changes so long as we bring more people into the experience and exercise.

Notes

1. Swift, Art. "Americans' Desire for Stricter Gun Laws Up Sharply." *Gallup.com*. 19 Oct. 2015. Web. <http://www.gallup.com/poll/186236/americans-desire-stricter-gun-laws-sharply.aspx>.

Lawful Immigrant and New Citizen Outreach

Ranjit Singh

I lived in the United States for several years as a legal non-immigrant foreign national before applying for lawful permanent resident (i.e., immigrant) status. When I finally received my green card in the mail, there was a flyer included with it that listed all my rights. One part was a short blurb about how I could own a firearm, though there was no other information besides that.

As time passed, I made one of the biggest decisions of my life, to become an American citizen. This was a particularly hard decision because the government of India does not recognize dual citizenship. Becoming an American meant renouncing my Indian citizenship and surrendering my Indian passport. After a lot of thought, I decided to move forward with the process.

When my naturalization papers were finally approved, I went to a federal court to take the oath of citizenship. That was an emotional moment. Keeping my stoic face intact and not breaking down in tears was a herculean effort. After I took the oath, I was greeted by the League of Women Voters who helped me register as a new voter.

My naturalization paperwork included some flyers, one of which also mentioned the right to own firearms in passing.

During this multi-year immigration and naturalization process, I received no communication or outreach effort from any of the major gun rights organizations in America. I do not fault them for this. These organizations are fighting tooth-and-nail to push back against the constant attacks on the Second Amendment. But more needs to be done, and it's up to all gun owners to get the message out.

What I would like to point out is that if I had not changed by mind on armed self-defense rights after the Mumbai terror attacks and voluntarily sought out firearms training, I would have still been the old me. I would have been naively comfortable with a government monopoly on guns and would have been demanding that gun ownership be restricted. Heck, I would have probably been a fan of Michael Bloomberg and would have quite possibly joined the mailing list of Everytown for Gun Safety and even donated money to them. What I find truly scary is that I would have been a *citizen* and a *voter* while holding these irrational hoplophobic views.

Every believer in the Second Amendment must understand that there are millions of the "old me" out there—immigrants from countries where the government has completely usurped the human right to armed self-defense and nudged the culture toward hoplophobia. As always, the children of these immigrants will assimilate quickly, but being raised in firearms-averse households, they will be less likely to know, understand, or care about firearms and the right to self-defense when they grow up and become voters.

There is a desperate need for outreach to immigrants and new citizens. This is quite possibly one of the best "Welcome to America" experiences that immigrants can get. I really wish one of my friends had reached out to me and taken me to the local range. Instead, I made these friends after I started researching firearms myself and signed up for an introductory course at the local range.

Large gun rights organizations like the NRA and Gun Owners of America should ideally lead or contribute significantly to outreach efforts targeted at immigrants and new citizens. This will dovetail nicely with their end goal of protecting the Second Amendment by broadening their base and improving overall public relations. As of 2010, over one out of eight people in America is foreign-born[1]. This is a sizeable portion of the population which can only be ignored at our own peril. And if those groups don't take the lead, each one of us will have to do it for them.

Notes

1. U.S. Census Bureau. "The Foreign-Born Population in the United States." *Census.gov*. 2010. Web. <https://www.census.gov/newsroom/pdf/cspan_fb_slides.pdf>.

What about the rest of the developed world?

Greg Camp

One of the frequent points raised by advocates of gun control is the lower homicide rates in other parts of the developed world. We're told endlessly about the peaceful societies of Britain, Australia, or Japan with the claim that the few murders—and especially fewer murders done with firearms—is the result of strict gun laws. This is treated as a devastating argument, but under analysis, the reality is complex, one that ultimately isn't even about guns.

The first thing to consider here is the actual rates in the United States and the other nations that get brought up and the pattern of such rates through history. Homicide rates have been dropping globally for a long time. This may feel completely wrong to anyone who watches the news, but as psychologist Steven Pinker demonstrated in his exhaustive work, *Better Angels of Our Nature*, deaths due to violence at the beginning of human civilization were in the hundreds per hundred thousand. These rates declined over the centuries to double digits and then below ten for the developed world throughout the 1900s. Despite the best efforts of murder mystery writers such as Agatha Christie and Colin Dexter to convince us otherwise, Britain's rate was under two per hundred thousand in the twentieth century. The same is true for Australia.

Here, gun control advocates tell us that the reason is the gun laws of those two nations. Gun registration began in Britain in the 20s out of fears that soldiers returning from World War I might get revolutionary ideas. More came in the 60s, and the handgun ban was enacted in 1997[1]. A similar history is found in Australia. And yet, in both nations, the homicide rates were basically constant, showing a gradual motion downward from close to two per hundred thousand to around one by the twenty-first century. At no point during the period did new gun laws cause any clear-cut decrease in the number of murders committed. It is true to say that Australia hasn't experienced a mass shooting on the order of America's experience since the gun laws passed after the Port Arthur massacre, though there have been several stabbing, shooting, and arson spree killings. What isn't often acknowledged is that New Zealand also hasn't had a mass shooting since 1996, and the Kiwis didn't impose new controls on legal gun ownership[2].

Japan offers another take on this subject. The Japanese homicide rate is famously low, and it's well known that ownership of firearms on that island has long been heavily restricted. But their suicide rate is far above America's. In absolute numbers, about as many Japanese kill themselves—not with firearms—as die by gunfire—regardless of whether we're talking homicide, suicide, or accident—in the United States[3]. And while summarizing a culture is tricky to do, it is safe to say that the Japanese put a much higher value on social conformity than we do[4].

Looking at Europe broadly, we can also make cultural observations. Class consciousness has deep roots going back over a millennium. Ownership of personal weapons has long been under rigid controls. At the end of the Middle Ages, knights covered themselves in thicker and thicker plate armor with the invention of firearms, and guns were seen as a destabilizing tool that belonged only in the hands of aristocrats and their authorized underlings. One point of contention, as discussed in José Ortega y Gasset's *Meditations on Hunting*, was the opportunity to take game, whether this would be the privilege of the upper class or a freedom available to all. But commoners in Europe have always been much less likely to own guns, and social ties of long standing put a brake on many kinds of violence. One contemporary concern has been the rise of fundamentalist terrorism and the wave of migration from the Middle East. Ordinary Europeans are increasingly wondering if taking defense into their own individual hands might be a good idea, and it remains to be seen how that will turn out.

But what about America? Our homicide rate is some four or five times Europe's countries, and about two-thirds of murders committed here are done with firearms. Of course, both the rates of Europe and the United States are very low when compared with the rest of the world. Mexico and Russia have homicide rates around three times ours, while South Africa experiences some thirty murders per hundred thousand people, and

Honduras suffers twice that rate[5]. In the United States, cities and states have highly variable rates, showing no correlation between gun deaths and gun laws[6]. The rate of murder in California is consistently within a decimal point of Texas, despite those two states having widely different regulations of guns. Louisiana has the most murders, while Vermont and New Hampshire have the fewest—and all three have laws that strongly support gun rights. New York City and Chicago both have long had strict gun control. The former has seen a significant drop in homicide since the peak in the early 90s, while the Second City remains one of the more violent in the nation.

As Pinker argues, there are measures that we can take to propel the downward trend in violence. He points to education, stable social institutions including the courts, and a reliable safety net as factors that make a nation more peaceful. One solution that looks obvious is to end the War on Drugs, a disastrous effort by law enforcement and the military to keep out substances that are in high demand by people caught in addiction. If we were to legalize or decriminalize drugs and treat their abuse as a public health matter instead of something to prosecute and punish, we'd take away the motivation of criminal gangs to kill each other over territory and the need of addicts to commit crimes to finance their expensive habit. If as a nation we also held schools at all levels with the same high regard that we do bombers and battalions, we'd solve many of the social ills that make a life of violence seem like the only option for too many in this country.

And yet we are currently caught in a debate between supporters of gun rights and supporters of gun control that makes further reductions in violence impossible. Supporters of control see their demands as the only answer, regardless of the evidence that making it more difficult for good people to own and carry firearms does nothing to reduce rates of homicide and other forms of violence. The real answer is in the improvement of social institutions, not in the curtailment of basic rights, and we gun owners have to hit that point home over and over until enough Americans move past desires for more control and work on what may appear to be soft solutions, but are in fact tested means of making a nation better.

Notes

1. BBC. "Britain's changing firearms laws." *BBC*. 12 Nov. 2007. Web. <http://news.bbc.co.uk/2/hi/uk_news/7056245.stm>.

2. McPhedran, Samara and Jeanine Baker. "Mass shootings in Australia and New Zealand: A descriptive study of incidence." *Justice Policy Journal*. Vol. 8, No. 1, Spring 2011. Web. <http://www.cjcj.org/uploads/cjcj/documents/Mass_shootings.pdf>.

3. "Suicide." *World Life Expectancy.com*. 2014. Web. <http://www.worldlifeexpectancy.com/cause-of-death/suicide/by-country/>.

4. Hogg, Chris. "'Forced confessions' in Japan." *BBC*. 29 Oct. 2007. Web. <http://news.bbc.co.uk/2/hi/asia-pacific/7063316.stm>.

5. "Violence." *World Life Expectancy.com*. 2014. Web. <http://www.worldlifeexpectancy.com/cause-of-death/violence/by-country/>.

6. "Murder Rates Nationally and By State." *Death Penalty Information Center*. 2016. Web. <http://www.deathpenaltyinfo.org/murder-rates-nationally-and-state>.

Towards a Left-Right Convergence on the Second Amendment

Ranjit Singh

If a single word can describe modern American politics, it is polarization. The country's political divide is getting wider as people dig in their heels over various issues. Guns are a divisive topic, and the rift between those supporting versus those opposing gun rights is only widening. This divide is manifesting itself in the two major political parties, as the Democratic Party gets more entrenched on gun control while the Republican Party favors more gun rights.

The Democratic Party traditionally did, and still does count gun owners among its big-tent coalition[1]. However, there is a clear build-up of an anti-gun rights posture within the party, which is marginalizing and will eventually drive out pro-gun rights Democrats[2]. This change threatens the long-term survival of the Second Amendment, because it increases the likelihood that when in power, the Democrats will do everything they can to erode this fragile freedom.

The political divide between the two dominant parties can be seen in the divergence in the fifty states on gun rights. Many states with Democratic majorities such as New York, California, Connecticut, and New Jersey have been gradually increasing their infringement on gun rights, whereas states where Republicans hold most offices such as Texas, Idaho, Montana, and Arizona have been increasing their citizens' free exercise.

Such divergence is obviously bad for gun owners in blue states, but in the long run will also threaten gun rights in states with Republicans in charge. As laws in the various states get challenged in courts and work their way up the judicial ladder, abuses of gun rights in one part of the country, if affirmed by the federal judiciary, will have ramifications in others.

As discussed earlier in this book, there is also the question of long-term socio-cultural effects. A handful of the most populous states attack gun rights, hobbling gun ownership and leading to an increase in ignorance among their residents. And it is from this gun-averse populace that future political and judicial leaders will be drawn. When such leaders end up at the federal level, gun rights will be imperiled even in those states that culturally and politically favor gun rights.

Therefore, it is important for gun owners not to write off the so-called blue states, the Democratic Party, and the Left as a whole. Despite policy differences in other areas, it is imperative that Republican, independent, and third-party gun owners offer their support to pro-gun rights Democrats, even though they seem to be a dying breed. The Democratic Party's hard line against gun rights must be softened, creating a bipartisan consensus on the subject.

Such convergence requires those supporting the Second Amendment to project a well-rounded message. Passion must be circumscribed by politeness, or the message will be lost at the slightest sign of abrasiveness. Contrast the intellectual rigor and politeness of former Secretary of State Condaleezza Rice, a self-professed Second Amendment absolutist[3], with the crass misogyny[4], racism[5], and anti-semitism[6] of NRA Board Member Ted Nugent.

It cannot be disputed that the pro-Second Amendment movement has, among its adherents, some loathsome bigots. This is true for any large movement or group like the Republican and Democratic Parties[7], the anti-Israel Boycott, Divestment, Sanctions (BDS) movement[8,9], and even the anti-Second Amendment gun control movement[10,11,12,13,14]. At the same time, it is undeniable that the pro-Second Amendment movement also counts black civil rights leaders[15,16], gays[17,18], Jews[19], and ethnic minorities[20,21] in its ranks. Alan Gura, the lead counsel for Dick Heller in the seminal *District of Columbia v. Heller* case is a Jewish Israeli-American[22]. Alan Gottlieb of the Second Amendment Foundation is Jewish. The Pink Pistols are a gun-rights organization for LGBT Americans and their allies. Given this, why the NRA has a repulsive person like Ted Nugent on its board is incomprehensible. It should be noted here that the NRA has a high favorability rating of 58%[23] among the American public, higher than both major-party 2016 presidential candidates[24,25]. But this high number is offset by a non-trivial unfavorable rating of 35%, which can be partly attributed to the antics of people like Nugent.

While it is all too easy to criticize the NRA, it is important to note why the organization is involved in legislative and judicial matters instead of focusing exclusively on its original mission of promoting marksmanship[26]. The NRA and other groups like Gun Owners of America and the Second Amendment Foundation defend the *only part* of the Bill of Rights that organizations like the ACLU refuse to defend[27,28]. That civil-rights organization, which has done commendable work in other areas, likes to pretend that the Second Amendment does not exist. Its position on the matter is jarring and incoherent[29,30]. While defending the Bill of Rights (minus the Second Amendment) and bending over backwards to fight for the unenumerated rights of people, which are sometimes called contrived rights by detractors, the group ignores the one enumerated, constitutionally-protected right that underwrites every other right, whether named explicitly or not. The ACLU's behavior is irresponsible and ignominious in this regard.

A Left-Right convergence on the Second Amendment should involve an all-out effort at achieving consensus *on the side of gun rights*. It must involve pervasive evangelism and sound messaging directed at the ignorant, with the end goals of winning over the Democratic Party and the American Left. We will know that such a consensus has been achieved when the ACLU joins the NRA as a passionate and tireless ally in defense of the Second Amendment. Until then, those who love freedom must not rest.

Notes

1. Silver, Nate. "Party Identity in a Gun Cabinet." The New York Times. 18 Dec. 2012. Web. <http://fivethirtyeight.blogs.nytimes.com/2012/12/18/in-gun-ownership-statistics-partisan-divide-is-sharp/?_r=0>.

2. "In Draft Party Platform, Democrats Regress on Gun Rights." *NRA-ILA*. 8 Jul. 2016. Web. <https://www.nraila.org/articles/20160708/in-draft-party-platform-democrats-regress-on-gun-rights>.

3. "Condoleezza Rice on Gun Control." *On The Issues*. Web. <http://www.ontheissues.org/Celeb/Condoleezza_Rice_Gun_Control.htm>.

4. Roberts, Michael. "Ted Nugent called Hillary Clinton a 'toxic c*nt'...eighteen years ago." *Westword*. 20 Apr. 2012. Web. <http://www.westword.com/news/ted-nugent-called-hillary-clinton-a-toxic-c-nt-eighteen-years-ago-5872607>.

5. Grow, Kory. "Ted Nugent Apologizes for Calling Obama a 'Subhuman Mongrel.'" *Rolling Stone*. 21 Feb. 2014. Web. <http://www.rollingstone.com/music/news/ted-nugent-apologizes-for-calling-obama-a-subhuman-mongrel-20140221>.

6. Bever, Lindsey. "Ted Nugent digs in amid anti-Semitic accusations — and calls for his NRA ouster." *The Washington Post*. 10 Feb. 2016. Web. <https://www.washingtonpost.com/news/post-nation/wp/2016/02/10/gun-rights-advocates-urge-nra-to-remove-ted-nugent-from-board-over-anti-semitic-outburst/?utm_term=.903a5eaa29c7>.

7. Silver, Nate and Allison McCann. "Are White Republicans More Racist Than White Democrats?" *FiveThirtyEight*. 30 Apr. 2014. Web. <http://fivethirtyeight.com/features/are-white-republicans-more-racist-than-white-democrats/>.

8. Neff, Blake. "Meet The Brilliant Harvard Student Who Called A Jewish Politician 'Smelly.'" *The Daily Caller*. 21 Apr. 2016. Web. <http://dailycaller.com/2016/04/21/meet-the-brilliant-harvard-student-who-called-a-jewish-politician-smelly/>.

9. Nagourney, Adam. "In U.C.L.A. Debate Over Jewish Student, Echoes on Campus of Old Biases." *The New York Times*. 5 Mar. 2015. Web. <http://www.nytimes.com/2015/03/06/us/debate-on-a-jewish-student-at-ucla.html?_r=0>.

10. Smith, Ben. "Obama on small-town Pa.: Clinging to religion, guns, xenophobia." *Politico*. 11 Apr. 2008. Web. <http://www.politico.com/blogs/ben-smith/2008/04/obama-on-small-town-pa-clinging-to-religion-guns-xenophobia-007737>.

11. Mullins, Melissa. "WashPost Op-Ed: The NRA Will Fall When Rural, Uneducated White People Die Off." *NewsBusters.org*. 22 Oct. 2015. Web. <http://newsbusters.org/blogs/nb/melissa-mullins/2015/10/22/washpost-op-ed-nra-will-fall-when-rural-uneducated-white-people>.

12. Farago, Robert. "Susie Madrak: At What Point Do We Shoot The Gun Nuts?" *The Truth About Guns*. 24 Jun. 2014. Web. <http://www.thetruthaboutguns.com/2014/06/robert-farago/susie-madrak-at-what-point-do-we-shoot-the-gun-nuts/>.

13. Savage One. "Breaking Through: How to Overcome the Stereotypical Imagery of Gun Ownership." *We Like Shooting.com*. 11 Nov. 2015. Web. <https://welikeshooting.com/blog/breaking-overcome-stereotypical-imagery-gun-ownership/>.

14. Rivera, Zayda. "Jim Carrey apologizes to assault rifle owners for past anti-gun comments: 'I'm sorry that in my outrage I called you names.'" *New York Daily News*. 8 Jul. 2013. Web. <https://www.nydailynews.com/entertainment/gossip/jim-carrey-gun-owners-outrage-called-names-article-1.1392868>.

15. Milloy, Courtland. "On MLK holiday, walking for civil rights and the Second Amendment." *The Washington Post*. 15 Jan. 2013. Web. <https://www.washingtonpost.com/local/on-mlk-holiday-walking-for-civil-rights-and-the-

16. Root, Damon. "A Forgotten Civil Rights Hero: The unappreciated legacy of entrepreneur-activist T.R.M. Howard." *Reason.com*. Apr. 2009. Web. <http://reason.com/archives/2009/03/20/a-forgotten-civil-rights-hero>.

17. Lee, Jessica. "A gay perspective on D.C. gun rights." *Washington Blade*. 22 Jul. 2010. Web. <http://www.washingtonblade.com/2010/07/22/a-gay-perspective-on-d-c-gun-rights/>.

18. Hsu, Spencer S. "Self-described 'peacenik' challenged D.C. gun law and won." *The Washington Post*. 8 Aug. 2014. Web. <https://www.washingtonpost.com/local/crime/self-described-peacenik-challenged-dc-gun-law-and-won/2014/08/08/d3d69acc-1cd7-11e4-82f9-2cd6fa8da5c4_story.html>.

19. Levy, Robert A. "A Victory for Self-Defense." *The Washington Post*. 12 Mar. 2007. Web. <http://www.washingtonpost.com/wp-dyn/content/article/2007/03/11/AR2007031101049.html?utm_term=.b35009805c46>.

20. "NRA Endorses Nikki Haley for Governor of South Carolina." *NRA-ILA*. 25 Sept. 2014. Web. <https://www.nrapvf.org/articles/20140925/nra-endorses-nikki-haley-for-governor-of-south-carolina>.

21. Corasanti, Nick. "Bobby Jindal Talks God and Guns at N.R.A. Forum." *The New York Times*. 10 Apr. 2015. Web. <http://www.nytimes.com/politics/first-draft/2015/04/10/bobby-jindal-talks-god-and-guns-at-n-r-a-forum/>.

22. Jewish Marksman. "Jewish Legal Minds and American Gun Rights: Gura, Sigale, Gottlieb, and Posner." *Jewish Marksmanship*. 29 Dec. 2012. Web. <http://jewishmarksmanship.blogspot.com/2012/12/jewish-legal-minds-and-american-gun.html>.

23. Swift, Art. "Despite Criticism, NRA Still Enjoys Majority Support in U.S." *Gallup.com*. 22 Oct. 2015. Web. <http://www.gallup.com/poll/186284/despite-criticism-nra-enjoys-majority-support.aspx>.

24. "2016 Candidate Favorability Ratings." *Real Clear Politics*. 2016. Web. <http://www.realclearpolitics.com/epolls/2016/president/favorable_unfavorable.html>.

25. Wright, David. "Poll: Trump, Clinton score historic unfavorable ratings." *CNN*. 22 Mar. 2016. Web. <http://www.cnn.com/2016/03/22/politics/2016-election-poll-donald-trump-hillary-clinton/>.

26. "A Brief History of the NRA." *NRA*. 2016. Web. <https://home.nra.org/about-the-nra/>.

27. "Second Amendment." *ACLU*. 2016. Web. <https://www.aclu.org/second-amendment>.

28. "FAQS." American Civil Liberties Union of Ohio. Web. <http://www.acluohio.org/about/faq>.

29. Blanks, Jeremy D. "The Hypocrisy of the ACLU." *Keep and Bear Arms*. 14 Aug. 2016. Web. <http://www.keepandbeararms.com/newsarchives/XcNewsPlus.asp?cmd=view&articleid=307>.

30. Blackman, Josh. "The ACLU's Abdication of the Second Amendment." *Josh Blackman's Blog*. 7 Dec. 2015. Web. <http://joshblackman.com/blog/2015/12/07/the-aclu-abdication-of-the-second-amendment/

Reaching Across the Divide

Greg Camp

Gun ownership and gun rights are subjects that many people treat like religion or politics, something not to be discussed at the dinner table, something not to talk about with strangers. But beliefs taken on faith and topics treated as taboo have the effect of reinforcing themselves through echoing, an effect that deepens the divide between groups.

How do we reach across and make a connection with people on opposing sides? This question has to be approached realistically. The first fact here is that some people cannot be reached. Time is a finite resource, and true believers in a cause will not change their minds or even consider facts that they are unable to process within their beliefs. The only purpose in talking to such people is if you're educating an audience in a debate. That is, unless you're having fun, but don't forget that this would be the sole point of the exercise.

True believers may be angry or otherwise driven by emotion. Such people have made so much of a commitment to the cause that they wrap their identities up in it and take any challenge to their beliefs as a personal insult.

Another type who is a waste of time is the kind of person who shows up only to derail adult conversation. The sure signs of people like this are rudeness, a refusal to address facts and logic directly, or a desire to play games rather than to engage seriously. On the Internet, they're known as trolls. Some are simply crude, while others are sophisticated in their ability to waste time, dragging out a conversation that keeps circling back to the beginning, no matter how many times questions have been answered and claims have been refuted. In either case, you'll get a sense of a person who isn't worth your time. Move on.

It's good to remember that these two types aren't the only people you'll meet. There are many people who can be reached. And here we get to the second fact. It's not your job to reach everyone. You're not saving souls, and while you might save lives, the good news about the United States is that we're a basically non-violent society. Gun ownership and carry are good things to improve the odds when done competently, but getting people to come into the gun community is more like monitoring a patient's weight and blood pressure, rather than trauma surgery. It's a good idea, but you don't have to be in a hurry.

With someone who's receptive, don't be a troll yourself. The Golden Rule is a moral principle that we can spend hour after hour trying to figure out, but it exists in so many cultures because it's a basically good idea. How would you like to be treated by someone who disagrees with you? If you wouldn't like a particular approach, it's probable that others won't like that, either. We on the gun rights side are often true believers ourselves, and opposition to a basic right that we support and engage in feels like a hateful act. But many people who are on the side of gun control are there because they really do want to save lives.

With that in mind, it's clear that we have to know the facts. The data are messy, but a strong argument can be made on the basis of facts that gun control offers no guarantee of safety or even any increased likelihood that violence will be reduced.

This is an essential point. We don't have to abandon the field when it comes to the subject of violence. The evidence from around the world shows a lack of correlation between gun laws and gun homicide rates[1], and that same lack of correlation remains true among American states[2]. What matters is levels of education, the success of government services, and the spread of opportunity among the population. And the good news in this regard is that since gun control is a position of the left-wing, we can demonstrate that left-wing solutions—schools, healthcare, and jobs programs—work, while gun control doesn't.

One point on the facts has to be clear. Don't drag in discussions of Hitler and the Nazis unless you're forced to deal with them, and don't get into the weeds of battling a hypothetically tyrannical American government. At least, don't be the one who introduces those topics to the discussion. Nazi Germany is a bad subject generally, since it was an extraordinary case of vast evil, and we can't really learn anything from the gun laws of that period other than to say that tyrannies are bad ideas. The concept of asymmetrical warfare against a tyranny is a subject that we can debate, but you should always be explicit that you don't want to fight in a civil war. It's the gun control side that keeps extolling the pleasures of our government attacking American gun owners, and you must keep hitting home the point that we don't want to kill anyone, nor do we want a bloody conflict that would tear this country apart.

Gun control advocates will bring these subjects up, though, and what this reveals is a third fact, namely that the argument is not solely about facts and logic alone. How a person feels about this topic will often be much more influential than logic will be. And swaying a person's emotions is something that we on the gun rights side too often forget.

How do we accomplish that? We have to show that gun ownership is something that contributes to safety when done well, but we also have to work with the American love of freedom. As a nation, we got our start on the principle that each person has inherent rights by virtue of being human. We failed to live up to this lofty assertion for a long time, and we still have work to do to realize this fully, but as a guiding concept, it's hard to come up with a better one.

The idea of inherent human rights is treated as passé by a lot of people trying to be trendy, but it's hard to be against the claim that each one of us deserves personal agency and autonomy and ought to respect those facts about everyone else. Gun control advocates will claim to support basic rights, while insisting that every right has limits and that owning or carrying guns really aren't rights at all. It's easy to compare gun rights with other rights—abortion, in particular, and that red herring will be dragged through many a good argument—but the key point is that if I'm not harming innocents, the essence of our way of doing things is that I should be free to carry on as I wish.

As said above, we can't reach everyone. But we can make connections with people who are willing to listen to new ideas, to think about things from a new point of view. With them, find a time to take them to the range. Give them the basics of safe handling, and let them try out your own guns, especially .22 Long Rifle firearms. A day at the range is good fun, and letting someone try out shooting in a low-pressure manner will do more for the side of gun rights than many hours of argument will often achieve.

Notes

1. "Gun homicides and gun ownership by country." *The Washington Post*. 17 Dec. 2012. Web. <http://www.washingtonpost.com/wp-srv/special/nation/gun-homicides-ownership/table/>.

2. "Murder Rates Nationally and By State." *Death Penalty Information Center*. 2016. Web. <http://www.deathpenaltyinfo.org/murder-rates-nationally-and-state>.

Four Rules of Gun Safety

These rules are adapted from the original statement of them given by firearms instructor, Jeff Cooper. Follow these rules, and you will save yourself a world of grief:

1. Treat all guns as loaded.
2. Never let the muzzle cover anything you are not willing to destroy.
3. Keep your finger off the trigger till your sights are on the target.
4. Identify your target and what is around and behind it.

A Non-Aggression Pledge for Trainees

We believe that violence *per se* is deplorable and reflective of the human condition in its current state. As time progresses, we hope that humanity becomes kindler and gentler and that the better angels of our nature guide us in our lives. In the absence of such a utopia, the best we can hope for is conflict avoidance, and if conflict does arise, to attempt to resolve such conflict without violence to the maximum possible extent. However, there will be situations where violence cannot be avoided, and in such cases, the proportionate, reactive use of violence in limited situations is justified.

Imparting knowledge of weaponry means that the recipient can use that knowledge for good or evil. There is no way to predict human behavior. However, to quell any concerns that a trainer may have, we have prepared a non-aggression pledge that a trainer may, or ideally should, require a trainee to take. This pledge is inspired by the Libertarian pledge:

> I solemnly [swear / affirm] that I will not use my
> knowledge of firearms to commit verbal or
> physical aggression, threaten, or initiate
> violence against another human being.

A Basic Armory

Greg Camp

Having read this book, if you weren't a gun owner before, perhaps you've been convinced that owning guns is a good idea. This is an important decision, one that has to make sense, to own or not to own, for yourself. If you've decided to become a gun owner, we welcome you to the gun community. You'll be expected to learn how to use guns appropriately and to handle them in a way that doesn't harm innocents. You've read this book, and we'd like to think that's a good start, but this isn't the end. Read other books—firearms instructor and police officer, Massad Ayoob, has several good introductions to the subject. He's one of many who have good advice. Along the way, find a gun store with friendly employees who will treat you with respect. Take a class. Take as many as your time and budget allow. Also, learn the laws of your city and state. While we all should work for greater freedom, breaking the laws through ignorance isn't the way to go about that.

What follows here is one suggestion about specific guns to get you started. This is not the only way to get going. If you look back at the path that I followed into this world, you'll see that these are lessons learned from experience, not wisdom beforehand.

The first gun to buy is chambered in .22 Long Rifle. This cartridge is used in handguns and rifles, and in fact, it's good to get both. The advantages in .22 LR are several. For one, the round produces low recoil and less noise. You should still wear hearing protection, but the gentler firing energy means that a new shooter can focus on trigger control, grip and stance, and aiming. In the same way that your first time playing the piano for an audience shouldn't be at Carnegie Hall, your first work with firearms shouldn't be an elephant gun.

There are various makes and models of .22s. You may wonder which are the best, and with no desire to be coy, the answer is that it depends. Guns are like clothes in the sense that you have to try them on, wear them for a bit, and see how they feel. If you have a friend who knows about guns, take that person shopping with you. Ask the sales people at the gun store to let you hold whatever looks good to you. Make sure they fit well in your hand—after learning what a good firing grip looks like—or in the case of the rifle how well it rests against your shoulder, while giving enough distance between your eyes and the sights. In handguns, you'll have a choice between a self-loading or semiautomatic pistol and a revolver. At this stage, either is as good as the other. If your budget allows, buy both.

In addition to the soft shooting qualities of the .22, both the ammunition and the guns tend to be cheaper than their bigger cousins. That means you can fire a lot more rounds for the same cost, and the more rounds you send down range, the better your chances are at getting good.

A .22 also has some practical uses for real work beyond just practice. It's a good round for small game, and it can be used in self-defense. This cartridge is a rimfire round—look it up as you learn about guns—which means that it isn't as reliable as centerfire ammunition, and its small caliber and low power makes it not as dependable in stopping a violent attacker, but no one wants to be shot, and if you've been practicing, you'll have found out how to put rounds where they need to go.

Once you've become comfortable with operating your .22s, it's time to move on to more powerful handguns. These will be guns that you can carry in public or use as defensive guns in your home. Even if you don't want to carry, take a class for a carry license. You'll learn a lot about gun handling, regardless of how much you put that knowledge into practice.

Handguns in this category fall into two categories, full-size and pocket model. Full-size can also be called compact, but the grip length of any gun in this group allows you to wrap three fingers around it—middle, ring, and pinkie. The mid-size, again often called compact, lets you get that grasp, while also being easier than the biggest varieties to conceal. A gun like this will be put into a holster on your belt, whether inside the waistband or outside, or in a shoulder holster. A good option here, in terms of caliber, is the 9mm. Others are also good, but they can be snappy or heavier in recoil. Go to a range that rents guns or go shooting with a gun-owning friend to try out different pistol cartridges. But the 9mm is often cheaper and softer, even though with modern hollow point ammunition, it's as good as bigger rounds, and it allows more rounds in the magazine of a semiautomatic handgun for the same size gun.

A pocket gun exists as a backup or as something that you slide into your pocket when you are running out for a quick errand or can't conceal something bigger. In this example, the .38 Special is the definitive revolver round. And a revolver makes sense in this application. Carrying in a pocket requires unfailing obedience to the rules, and a semiautomatic can be less forgiving. By contrast, a double-action revolver has a trigger that takes deliberation to activate. You'll hear people advocating the .357 Magnum as a better round, and it is more powerful, but with greater power comes greater recoil and noise. The .38 Special is like the 9mm in that it is effective in modern ammunition, but is also easier to control.

As with the .22s, there are many examples of good handguns in these categories. Since these will be practical weapons and not just learning tools, look at reviews, read discussion boards, and watch YouTube videos about any make and model you are considering. As with cars, guns have reputations, often deserved, for reliability or otherwise, and you want a gun that works every time—or at least as many times as the best machines can work. Failures are part of the reason a backup gun is a good thing.

If you take a concealed carry class, in most states, you'll have a shooting test. Use a semiautomatic for that. If you use a revolver, in many states, you'll be limited to carrying only revolvers.

As good as they are, there is one brand of gun you shouldn't start out with: Glock. Don't misunderstand this. Glocks are good guns. They have safeties, most of which are internal. The one on the outside is on the trigger itself, which is the equivalent of putting the parking brake release on the accelerator. This may sound bad, but it is actually a reasonable choice for someone who has spent enough time to know how to handle guns instinctively. You may get to Glocks eventually, and you'll probably be pleased with them when you get there, but give yourself time to gain skills and confidence first.

Return now to long guns. Once you've learned how to handle the .22 rifle, it's time to get a shotgun and a centerfire rifle. Consider the shotgun first.

Shotguns are excellent guns for hunting and for self-defense. Given the multiple types of shells that they use, you can take birds, deer, or hogs. In self-defense, a twelve gauge buckshot round sends typically nine pellets of about the diameter of a 9mm pistol round down range—and yes, they do have to be aimed, though the longer barrel makes doing that easier to do in some ways. The twelve gauge is powerful, while the twenty gauge is gentler on the shoulder. Don't bother with other gauges unless you inherited a sixteen or similar from grandpa. Twelve and twenty are the most common, and thus are the cheapest and most likely shells to find in the store. As with other guns, shop around, feel how the shotgun fits. See if you want a pistol grip or a grip like a rifle's. See what length of barrel is best for your size. The old top-break double-barrel guns will cost a lot of money, so go with a pump action or a semiautomatic. The latter offers less recoil, since the force of the shell firing is used by the mechanism to cycle the action.

This leaves rifles. Here we have a whole separate world of variety. If you plan to hunt, find out what rounds are best for the game you will pursue. Any centerfire rifle round will be effective against a human attacker. Clint Smith, one of the best known gun instructors, says that a handgun is what you use to fight your way back to the rifle you should never have put down. We put rifles down because they're big, impractical to carry in ordinary living, but when we fetch them, we have a weapon that is capable of dealing with a lot of situations. As the poem by Lindy Wisdom—daughter of one of the founders of modern thinking about guns, Jeff Cooper—puts it, there aren't many problems a person can't fix with $700 and a .30-'06. Or a .308. Or a .270. Or....

Rifles reach out. They let you exert force at a distance. They require lots of practice to operate well. If you're not a hunter, you may care more about a smaller carbine, a shorter rifle, for personal defense. As discussed in the chapter on assault rifles, the U.S. military went with the AR-15, a carbine chambered in .223 caliber, in the 60s, and the Soviet Bloc chose the AK-47 in a reduced power .30 caliber round. Those are good rifle rounds if you're primarily interested in dealing with attackers trying to harm you.

At this point, you're deep in what the gun blogger, Kim du Toit, called the gun nut forest. You may be satisfied with this basic armory, or you might find that you want to expand your collection into a blossoming variety of makes, models, and calibers. In all of this, in addition to the practical benefits and the safety considerations, remember to have fun. Taking your guns to the range and shooting paper or soda bottles is a satisfying afternoon, even on the days when you feel you couldn't shoot your foot if the gun were taped to your shoe. Shooting well is a skill, one that takes time and dedication to learn. It's also a good time. The thump and bang of firearms can be as joyful as a fireworks display or Beethoven's *Ninth Symphony*. So if you've decided to join the gun community, welcome. It's a grand experience, one that's likely to be fulfilling and rewarding.

Epilogue

This has been a quick look at the gun community, gun ownership, and gun rights. This subculture has many highways and byways, and you can spend a lifetime in it and not experience the totality. We've given you a brief greeting, handed you a drink, and sent you into the party to get to know everyone.

If you're new to this community, welcome. If you've been with us for a while now, how many of your fellow Americans have you invited to join us? How many times have you held your own in an argument about gun rights? How many articles on news sites about guns have you commented on, how many politicians have you declared your support for gun rights to, and how many of your fellow gun owners have you taken to the polls to vote for our interests?

We all have work to do. Rights only survive in each generation when people of good will refuse to allow the fearful, the controlling, and the greedy to violate them. If rights are as important to you as they are to us—Ranjit Singh and Greg Camp—get out there and bring more people in to our side. Each one of us has this job to do. We can't leave that to someone else.

Each one, teach one. It's the way we win.

Ranjit Singh and Greg Camp

Appendix: Political spectra

Greg Camp

Throughout this book, we have been playing along with the standard spectrum from left to right in political orientation, but this requires some analysis. Spend time discussing politics with people who think independently, and you will find that they hold some ideas that are not in line with the party platforms of the Democrats or Republicans. Insisting on left and right and points in between forces a compression of positions into a single dimension that creates the appearance, but not the reality of big-tent major parties. As will be explained here, this erases real differences, thereby confusing an understanding of political philosophy.

Left and right wings originate in the time of the French Revolution. Monarchists sat on the right side of the Estates

General, the French parliament, while the Republicans, the party in favor of removing the monarchy and establishing the leadership of the people, took their seats on the left[1]. From this seating chart, we get our associations of the right wing with traditionalism or conservatism and the left with radicalism or liberalism. But when we are not in moments of national emergency, such simplistic divisions do not feel so urgently necessary.

Consider the supposed opposites of liberal and conservative. Liberal has been twisted out of its roots to mean basically Democrat, but the origin of the word is *liber*, Latin for free. Classical liberalism, as developed in the Enlightenment by John Locke and many others, was concerned with concepts of individual rights and the consent of the governed. In essence, this is a devotion to liberty for everyone. Conservatism suggests keeping—conserving—what we have. To see how liberalism and conservatism are not by nature opposites, consider how a conservationist—someone who wishes to preserve the environment, including biological diversity—are often on the left wing of American politics.

In fairness, we must note that conservatism can refer to the continuation of a set of supposedly traditional values such as marriage being restricted to one man and one woman or the status of Christianity as the definitive religion of the United States. This, however, often depends on a constructed past, since in many cases what people assume they are preserving was never actually the case.

The problem here is that people want to be regarded as liberal or conservative and end up having to shoehorn their beliefs into what are in fact positions of political philosophy, while those beliefs have been arrived at through some other means. By the definitions used in this writing, a liberal can be a conservative. Which is to say, a person can believe that individual liberties must be conserved.

For the sake of clarity, consider a two-dimensional plane, rather than a single linear spectrum. On this plane, call the x-axis conservative on the left vs. radical on the right and the y-axis liberal at the top and authoritarian at the bottom.

Radical comes again from the Latin word, *radix*, meaning root. It also meant radish. The idea here is that the radical wants to root out things as they are to replace them with some new system or condition, and thus is someone on the other end of a line from conservatives. Authoritarian is probably obvious, but just to be clear, this is the belief in the concentration of power in the hands of the one leader or a political elite.

What about progressivism? This is a politically created term, since few are opposed to genuine progress—though not few enough, it seems at times. But if the term has an objective meaning, it must be someone who supports or promotes change for the purpose of making things better. The progressive, then, is in between conservatives and radicals in that progressivism in this sense is an evolutionary, rather than radical change—change that accumulates over time and that preserves the gains that are made.

With these clarifications in mind, the following graph—inspired by the work of David Nolan, one of the founders of the Libertarian Party—is a more persuasive means of locating a person's political position:

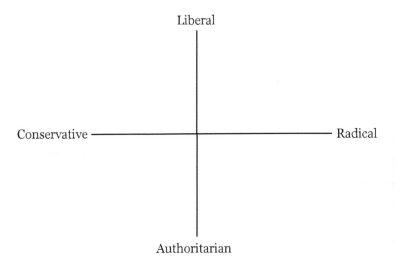

We can thus find the region into which this book falls—namely high on the y-axis. The core of the gun-rights argument is that each of us has inherent rights—the liberal position—and that these include the rights to own property and to defend our lives. As discussed in the chapter on the origin of rights, this logically includes the right to own and carry guns.

Notes

1. "Is The Economist left- or right-wing?" *The Economist*. 2 Sept. 2013. Web. <http://www.economist.com/blogs/economist-explains/2013/09/economist-explains-itself-0>.

Suggested Reading

Cooper, Jeff. *To Ride, Shoot Straight, and Speak the Truth.* Boulder, CO: Paladin, 1998. Print.

—. *The Art of the Rifle.* Boulder, CO: Paladin, 1997. Print.

Hamilton, Alexander, John Jay, and James Madison. *The Federalist.* New York: Modern Library, 1937. Print.

Hitchens, Christopher. *Thomas Jefferson*: Author of America. New York: Harper Collins, 2005. Print.

—. *Why Orwell Matters.* New York: MJF Books, 2002. Print.

Jefferson, Thomas. *Notes on the State of Virginia.* Ed. William Peden. New York: Norton, 1982. Print.

Okrent, Daniel. *Last Call*: The Rise and Fall of Prohibition. New York: Scribner, 2010. Print.

Index

.22 Long Rifle, 12, 14, 158, 163 – 164
.270, 167
.30-'06, 167
.308, 167
.357 Magnum, 165
.38 Special, 165
.40 Smith & Wesson, 14
3-D printing, 16, 110
8mm Lebel, 92
9mm Luger, 165
9/11 attack, 5, 20
1984, 122
Abbate, Anthony, 106
Abortion, 11, 82
ACLU, 122, 147
Aeneid, The, 65
Age of Enlightenment, 14, 172
Ai Weiwei, 122
AK-47, 95, 98
Ambedkar, Bhimrao, 73
Appalachian Trail, 12
AR-15, 95, 98
Arizona, 145
Armenian genocide, 83
Assault Weapon, 32
Atlantic, The, 109
Aurora, Colorado attack, 30
Australia, 138 – 139
Automatic—fully automatic, semiautomatic, 32, 33, 97
Ayoob, Massad, 162
Baghdad, Siege of, 75
Baker, Peter, 40
Beer, invention of, 65
Beethoven, Ludwig von, 167
Belgian Congo, 107
Beretta, 14
Beslan school attack, 5, 75
Better Angels of Our Nature, 139
Bill of Rights, 7, 23, 54, 78 – 79, 123
Black Powder, 14
Bloomberg, Michael, 83, 135
Bolt action rifle, 5, 92 – 93
Breyer, Stephen, 33
Browne, Carol, 60
Bush, George W., 108, 122
California, 31, 141, 145

Each One, Teach One

Canada, 12
Caste system, 74
Charleston attack, 105, 109
Charleston loophole, 105 – 106'
Chattanooga recruitment center attack, 103
Chhatrapati Shivaji Terminus, 5
Chicago, 106, 141
China, 81, 82, 122
Citizens United, 123, 124
Clinton, Hillary, 105
Clip, 30, 31
Colbert, Stephen, 122
Collins, Amanda, 60 – 61
Colorado, 30, 60
Colt, Sam, 16
Colt Single Action Army, 64
Connecticut, 145
Conservatives, 14, 17, 172
Constitution, 7, 125
Cooper, Jeff, 12, 14, 160, 167
Cowperthwaite, John, 82
Cruz, Ted, 39
Danbury, Connecticut Baptists, 20
Declaration of Independence, 20, 73, 79
DeGette, Diana, 30
de Leon, Kevin, 31
de Menezes, Jean Charles, 6
Democrats, i, 15, 30, 31, 60, 105, 144, 145, 146, 171
Deng Xiaoping, 82
Department of Defense, 84
Diana (Roman goddess), 65
Dihydrogen monoxide, 29
Doordarshan, 123
Drones, 6
Drug Enforcement Agency, 107
du Toit, Kim, 14, 167
Einstein, Albert, 11
Eliot, T.S., 64
Everytown for Gun Safety, 135
Federal Bureau of Investigation, 105
Feral hogs and AR-15, 98
Fernandez, Yvan, 108
First Amendment, 13, 23, 78, 109, 124
Florida, 108
Fourth Amendment, 79
France, 121
Franklin, Benjamin, ii
Freedom of Information Act, 79
French Revolution, 171
Freud, Sigmund, 63
Frum, David, 108 – 109
Fullerton, California, 85
Garissa College attack, 6
Geller, Pamela, 108
Georgia, State of, 85
Germany, 121

Index

Gerson, Michael, 109
Ghost gun, 31
Gibson Guitar, 85
Ginsburg, Ruth Bader, 33 – 34
Giron, Angela, 31
Gizmodo, 39
Glock, 107, 165 – 166
Google, 110
Google News, 43
Gottlieb, Alan, 146
Greens, i
Gun Owners of America, 136, 147
Gura, Alan, 146
Gurley, Akai, 106 – 107
Handguns, 99, 164
Healthcare, 12
Heller, 31 – 32
Heller, Dick, 146
History Channel, 13
Hitchens, Christopher, 24
Ho Chi Minh, 73
Hollow point bullets, 6
Honduras, 141
Hong Kong, 82
Hoplophobia, 42, 107, 108, 129, 131, 135
Hudak, Evie, 31, 60 – 61
Huffington Post, The, 39
Hurricane Katrina, 85, 107
Idaho, 145
India, 3, 4, 7, 44, 73, 74, 75, 110, 121, 122, 132
Indian Army, 6
Intermediate cartridge, 94 – 95
Internal Revenue Service, 80, 81
IRNA, 122
ISIS, 103
Isla Vista attack, 110
Islam, 20, 108, 121
Japan, 44, 138, 139 – 140
Jefferson, Thomas, 21 – 22, 73
Joe the Plumber, 80
Jones, Terry, 108
Journal News, The, 81
Kagan, Elena, 33 – 34
Kalashnikov, Mikhail, 95
Kashmir, 6
Lakhvi, Zaki ur Rehman, 4
Landler, Mark, 40
Lashkar-e-Toiba, 4
League of Women Voters, 135
Lemon, Don, 39
Lenin, Vladimir, 130
LGBT, 146
Liberals, 7, 11, 14, 15, 16, 17, 33, 172, 174
Libertarians, i, 161, 173
Limbaugh, Rush, 122
Locke, John, 172
Louisiana, 141

Luger P08, 13
M-16, 95
M1911, 16, 64
McCarthy, Carolyn, 29
McDonald, 32
Madison, James, 7, 74
Mad minute, 93
Madrid train bombings, 6
Magazine capacity, 30, 31
Markley's Law, 63
Marriage equality, 12, 19
Mauser Gewehr 98, 93
Meditations on Hunting, 140
Mexico, 140
Miami-Dade, 108
Microaggressions, 52
Militia, 32, 74 – 75, 76, 85
Mill, John Stuart, 22
Minerva (Roman goddess), 65
Minnesota, 80
Montana, 145
Mosin-Nagant, 16
Morse, John, 30
Mosque, 20
Mumbai terror attack, 3, 4, 5, 6, 7, 75
Murfreesboro, Tennessee, 21
Nanking, Rape of, 75
Napoleonic Wars, 92
Nashville, Tennessee, 41
National Geographic, 20

National Guard, 85
National Security Agency, 80
New Delhi, 5
New Hampshire, 141
New Jersey, 60, 145
New York, 81 – 82, 105, 145
New York City, 21, 34, 83, 106, 107
New York Times, The, 30, 40 – 42
New Zealand, 139
Newtown, Connecticut attack, 30, 33
Ninth Amendment, 23
Ninth Symphony, 167
Nolan, David, 173
Notes on the State of Virginia, 22
NPR, 123
NRA, 39, 42, 130, 136, 146, 147
Nugent, Ted, 146
NY SAFE Act, 103 – 105
Obama, Barack, 33, 40, 80, 101, 122
Obergefell, 19
Office of Personnel Management, 81
Ohio, 80
Ortega y Gassett, José, 140
Orwell, George, 122
Paige, Lee, 107

Pakistan, 4
Paris attack, Nov. 2015, 6, 75
passive voice in gun reporting, 42
PBS, 123
Pena, Michael, 106
Pink Pistols, 146
Pinker, Steven, 139, 141
Pravda, 122
Prohibition, 43
Reed, Dan, 5
Reilly, Ryan J., 39
Religion, 12, 20, 21
Remington New Model Army 1858, 14
Republicans, i, 108, 122, 144, 145, 146, 171
Revolver, 12, 14
Rice, Condaleezza, 146
Rushdie, Salman, 121
Russia, 140
Rwandan genocide, 43 – 44
Safe spaces, 52
Sagan, Carl, 11
San Bernardino attack, 41
Satanic Verses, The, 121
Second Amendment, 7, 12, 23, 34, 42, 78, 108, 109, 125, 127, 130, 132, 135, 145, 146, 147
Second Amendment Foundation, 146, 147
Separation of church and state, 21
Seventh Amendment, 20
Seventh-day Adventism, 12
Short Magazine Lee Enfield, 93
Shoulder thing that goes up, 29
Shotgun, 166
Sikkim, 44
Siler, Wes, 39
Six Amendments: How and Why We Should Change the Constitution, 32
Smith, Clint,   166
Socarras, Dario, 108
Sotomayor, Sonya, 33 – 34
South Africa, 140
South Korea, 107
Springfield 1903, 93
State of the Union, 109
Steed, Lisa, 107
Stevens, John Paul, 31 – 32, 97
Stewart, John, 122
Stoner, Eugene, 95
Sturmgewehr 1944, 94
Submachine gun, 93 – 94
Sugarmann, Josh, 96
Suicide, 44
Supreme Court, 33
Special Weapons And Tactics, 85

Taj Hotel, 6
Tales of the Gun, 13
Tennessee, 13
Terror in Mumbai, 5
Texas, 141, 145
Thatcher, Margaret, 58
Third Amendment, 85
Thompson submachine gun, 94
Trigger warnings, 52
Umpqua Community College attack, 101
Unek, William, 107
United Kingdom, 138 – 139
United Nations, 54
United States Constitution, 73
Universal Declaration of Human Rights, 54
University of Virginia, 21
Varela, Omaree, 108
Vermont, 141
Vilks, Lars, 108
Violence Policy Center, 96 – 97, 98, 99
Virgil, 65
War on Drugs, 141
Warren v. District of Columbia, 103
Wayne, John, 64
Weapons of mass destruction, 109
Weimar Republic, 83
Weinberg, Steven, 11
West, Kanye, 122
Westergaard, Kurt, 108
Westgate shopping mall attack, 6, 75
Winchester 1892, 64
Woo Bum-kon, 107
Woodworking, 13
Xinhua, 122

Greg Camp was born in the hills of North Carolina about a hundred thirty years later than was good for him. He has wandered around the southern United States ever since, picking up bits of experience and polishing his curmudgeonly persona. He listens to the Muses whenever they sing to him. Following a star brought him and his cats to northwest Arkansas, where he has found safe harbor.

gregcampnc@gmail.com

@gregcampnc

https://englreadingandwriting.wordpress.com/

Ranjit Singh is a father, husband, Indian immigrant, and naturalized citizen of the United States. An irredeemable nerd and polyglot with varied interests, Singh has wandered around and lived in a dozen cities. When not spending time with family, he likes to catch up on reading and occasionally write.

Ranjit.Singh.Author@gmail.com

@AuthorSingh

Made in the USA
Coppell, TX
23 May 2020